A PRACTICAL GUIDE TO KINGDOM EDUCATION

HOW TO TEACH BIBLICAL CURRICULUM IN THE HOME, CHURCH, OR PUBLIC SCHOOL

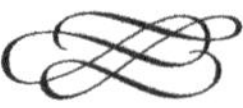

NANCY HAMELOTH ED.D.

CONTENTS

Acknowledgments vii

1. Introduction 1
2. What Is Kingdom Education? 5
3. The Kingdom View of the Child 11
4. Philosophy of Kingdom Education 15
5. Do Academic Results Matter? 19
6. Biblical Methodology 25
7. How to Develop Curriculum 35
8. Kingdom Curriculum Applied 65
9. Relationship-Building Principles 69
10. How Do I Begin? 109
11. What Should We Be Evaluating? 117
12. Sample Overviews, Lesson Plans, Templates, and Tools 121

Blank Yearly Review 123
Quarterly Plan 124
Unit Overview 125
Lesson Plan 128
Key Individual Chart 129
Self-Evaluation 130
Kingdom Concept Chart 131
Christian School Sample 132
Quarterly Plan Sample Themes 133
Quarterly Plan 134
Unit Overview 135
Kingdom Education Weekly Schedule Sample 138
Lesson Plan 140
Self-Evaluation 141
Dr. Claudia Berry's Kingdom Research 143
Dr. Cox's Research on Kingdom Education 191
Principle Approach Education 195
Kingdom of Heaven Scriptures 209
Kingdom of God Scriptures 215
Thy Kingdom Come – Prayer Principles 225
Resources 235
About the Author 243
Next Steps 245

ACKNOWLEDGMENTS

Although this book was written by me, it would not have been possible without the loving input of so many lives. I thank God for every person who has touched my life and taken the time to pour into me. I have been blessed with many faithful friends, prayer warriors, and mentors over the years.

First, I would like to thank my precious family once again for loving and supporting me through prayers and encouragement throughout my lifelong journey. Their love and support make it possible for me to live and grow in my Christian walk. Thank you, Susie for being a sister-friend. I love you so much and treasure our times of prayer and sharing together. Thank you, DJ, for being an amazing woman of God, who is not ashamed of the gospel and is transparent through your struggles and your victories. You are truly a daughter that brings praise to your Mother by your life (Proverbs 31). Thank you, Mike, for being steadfast in your hope of the gospel, even when times are hard. You are a mighty man of God and He has greater things in store for you than you will ever know.

Second, I would like to acknowledge my many friends from Stonebridge School and the Foundation for American Christian Education.

Dr. Max Lyons has been a lifelong friend, mentor, and confidant over the years and I would not be where I am today without his believing in me so many years ago and introducing me to the Principle Approach™. Thanks Max and Margie!

Third, I would like to thank Dr. William F. Cox, Jr. who gave me the chance to teach at Regent University in the Christian School Program. He helped me through many tough times and believed in me and helped push me beyond what I thought possible. His faithful mentorship of so many will only be acknowledged fully in the Kingdom to come.

Fourth, I would like to acknowledge Dr. Elizabeth Youmans and Chrysalis International for her love and support over the years. Elizabeth helped train me at Stonebridge School and beyond as she sent me on many mission trips to train international friends in Biblical, Christian education. She has been a true and loyal prayer warrior and friend.

Fifth, I want to acknowledge my dear friend Dr. Claudia Berry, who has been faithful to pray with me weekly throughout this journey. She has a heart for kingdom education, prayer, and intercession like no one else I know. She is full of wisdom and insight and I treasure our friendship in the Lord.

Last, I want to acknowledge my new friends at Self-Publishing School. This book would still just be an unfinished manuscript if it weren't for their dedication to help each student succeed.

May God richly bless you all for all your help, love, and support!

DEDICATION

This book is dedicated to the glory of God! God has taken me on an amazing journey of learning beyond what I could ever have dreamed and I dedicate this book to Him and to all my fellow pilgrims on the journey of life-long learning. May the God of all wisdom guide you and fill you with His love as you hear the high calling to train yourself as a laborer who is not ashamed, rightly dividing the Word of truth (2 Timothy 2:15).

Also, I dedicate this book to my loving family for their support throughout this journey. Truly God has blessed me with the love of two grown children, Deborah Joy Hastings and Michael David Hameloth. They are a blessing to me as I see them walking in God's ways and training their own children to live for God too. I also want to dedicate it to my precious grandchildren: Noah, Zachary, Ellison, and, soon to come, Virginia Jean. May all your children be taught of the Lord and great will be the peace of your children (Isaiah 54:13). My prayer is that many children will come into the Kingdom as a result of this book and I dedicate it to them as well.

Finally, I want to dedicate this book to my wonderful prayer partner Dr. Claudia Berry. She has been faithful to pray with me and support this work from its conception to its completion and I couldn't have done it without her.

I also thank the Lord for all the mentors and friends I have made at Stonebridge School, the Foundation for American Christian Education, Chrysalis International, Regent University, and all those I have had the privilege of teaching at home and abroad. May this book bring glory to God's kingdom worldwide.

But seek ye first the kingdom of God, and his righteousness; and all these things shall be added unto you.

—Matthew 6:33

INTRODUCTION

Who Is This Book Written For?

This book was written to address the need for Kingdom education for the lay person. It is written by a professional with over thirty years classroom experience for the person who has little or no experience. The goal is that the vision would be written so plainly that anyone could pick it up and begin teaching Kingdom concepts without any specialized training. It was written particularly for the body of Christ worldwide, many of whom will never be able to leave home for a formal education but are willing to start small by teaching their own children or others who want to learn more about living for the King. It is purposely simple so that it can be easily understood and followed without a lot of materials, just a prayerful and willing heart and the Word of God. If this is you, keep reading.

What Is in This Book?

This book will rely heavily on Scripture, since it is our guidebook for life and can be accessed in every language. It is written in response to the biblical mandate to train our children in God's ways. Deuteronomy 11:18, 19 says,

Therefore you shall lay up these words of mine in your heart and in your soul, and bind them as a sign on your hand, and they shall be as frontlets between your eyes. You shall teach them to your children, speaking of them when you sit in your house, when you walk by the way, when you lie down, and when you rise up.

It begins with a relationship with the loving God of the universe and is a method of passing on His precepts to our children and grandchildren. It will deal with large issues like philosophy, methodology, curriculum, and evaluation, but in such a way that they will be easily understood and mastered by anyone with a willing and teachable heart. It will also include practical tools like overviews, lesson plans, assessments, and access to many resources. The goal is that you use this as a beginning point to develop your own enriched biblical curriculum using whatever starting point you have at hand. If you are required to use a standardized curriculum, I will show you how to make it Kingdom rich. If you have nothing, I will show you how to begin. If you are happy with a Christian curriculum already, then this book is not for you. If you are searching for something more, then join me on this journey of discovery. I guarantee it will be an enriching experience for you and all those you touch for the Kingdom.

How Should I Use This Book?

This book is an introduction to Kingdom education. You should continue to study Scriptures and ask the Holy Spirit to direct your path. He is the teacher of teachers and will lead you into all truth. It is a resource, but I will also recommend many other books and websites that might help you further. The goal is that you have a beginning place to start a lifelong journey of learning. I pray that it will excite you to the possibility that you too can be a teacher. I pray that you will use the gifts God has given you to start Christian schools all over the world. Start small. God always starts with a remnant to change nations. May you be a part of the next great awakening in Kingdom education.

WHAT IS KINGDOM EDUCATION?

To begin the study of Kingdom education we should start by understanding what is meant by the word *kingdom*. Noah Webster in his 1828 *American Dictionary of the English Language* defines kingdom as "The territory or country subject to a king"; "The inhabitants or population subject to a king"; and "In Scripture, the government or universal dominion of God." It also can refer to Heaven (Matt 5:3); the reign of the Messiah (Mal 3) or God's people themselves as stated in Exodus 19:6, "You shall be unto me a kingdom of priests." Jesus taught extensively about the Kingdom of God, as did the apostles and other New Testament writers. I would recommend you begin a personal study of the Kingdom of God using the Blue Letter Bible, which is a great research tool available online and free of charge (www.blueletterbible.org).

Briefly defined, we find that the Kingdom of God is both here and now and coming in its fullness when Christ returns (Mark 1:15; 9:1; Luke 13:29; 17:20, 21). It is every true believer who has submitted to the Lordship of Christ (Rom 14:17; I Cor 4:20). It is open to all who receive Christ (John 3:3, 5; Luke 6:20). We become citizens of God's kingdom at rebirth and learn more about how to become faithful to the teachings of Christ throughout our lifetime, so it is a lifelong pursuit (Acts 14:22). Kingdom citizens are called apart to live a holy life separated from the world (I Cor 6:9, 10; 15:50). The Kingdom of God is a paradox: it is so simple that a child can enter, yet it is beyond understanding fully in this lifetime; it is here and now, yet coming fully at Christ's return; and it is entered into by faith in the finished work of Christ on the cross.

Next, we need to look at the word *education*. Webster's 1828 dictionary at http://websters dictionary1828.com defines it as

> *noun* [Latin educatio.] The bringing up, as of a child, instruction; formation of manners. *Education* comprehends all that series of instruction and discipline which is intended to enlighten the understanding, correct the temper, and form the manners and habits of youth, and fit them for usefulness in their future stations. To give children a good *education* in manners, arts and science, is important; to give them a religious *education* is indispensable; and an immense responsibility rests on parents and guardians who neglect these duties.

Education is so much more than relaying facts and focusing on the things of this earth only; it is preparing students for life in the Kingdom of God. It involves "correcting the temper" and "forming the manners and habits of youth." Our goal is to bring students into a relationship with the King of the Universe and allow His Spirit to do a deep work in their lives.

Dr. William F. Cox, professor at Regent University, states it this way:

> Broadly, a kingdom reflects the characteristics of its king. Accordingly, God's kingdom is primarily about God's essential nature of love. His kingdom is about joy-filled relationships within a harmonious family of an eternal Father who lavishly loves his children. In adoring the Father, biblical obedience of his sons and

> daughters originates affectionately rather than dutifully. The love-based Two Greatest Commandments and the Great Commission coupled with the power qualities of the Holy Spirit capture the essence of God's Kingdom on earth. This kingdom of agape love and power is matched by the fact that humans were created to love and be loved, a prime reflection of God's image. (Cox, 2013, p.3)

When we talk about God's Kingdom, we will be referring to living in relationship with the God of the universe through the substitutionary death of Jesus Christ. We will be applying these principles in an academic setting, but we are primarily about relationships, first with God and then with each other as expressed in the two greatest commandments (Matt 22:36-40).

Dr. Cox gives some practical examples of what kingdom education should look like.

> Kingdom education focuses on treating self and others as forgiven just as God does (Col 2:13) – sinner identity no more; believers are saints! The focus is on, for instance, uncovering the God-implanted 'gold' in humans' earthly natures, operating in the supernatural, 'going the extra mile,' loving unconditionally, eliminating judgmental attitudes, receiving inner healing, living as kingdom royalty, praying powerfully, establishing a culture of honor, desiring and enjoying God's presence, joyfully trusting God in all things, learning to live responsibly in liberty, pursuing personal destiny from God, being completely preoccupied with God, naturally exuding Sermon on the Mount and fruit of the Spirit qualities, being instruments of healing, evangelizing the lost, blessing others, living in gratitude and gratefulness, praising and worshipping God, expecting Kingdom visitations, living from heaven's abundance rather than earth-bound neediness, disciplining rather than punishing, banishing shame, and hearing God's voice. The focus is intimate fellowship with God, blessing and honoring his heart rather than performing obediently for him. (Cox, 2013)

The emphasis is on making disciples by bringing our students into a living, loving relationship with God. They are born again and growing in their walk with Christ. They are united in love as part of the body of Christ and growing as true disciples. They are about the Kingdom business of winning the lost and healing the sick, binding the brokenhearted, etc. (Luke 4:18). "Kingdom Education can be described as being Spirit-empowered, living in agape love with God, self and others to partner with the Creator of the universe to live from heaven to earth" (Cox, 2013).

When we typically think of Christian education, we think of a secular education with some Bible verses added. In this book, we are describing a radical shift in that thinking. We want to change the emphasis from focus on success in this temporal life to living in and for the Kingdom of God. While students will be taught academically, the emphasis will be on training them to live so radically different from the world that the academics become secondary to the goal of making disciples for Christ and ushering in His Kingdom.

> Descriptions of what the kingdom looks like on earth include that it is of power (1 Cor 4:20) and love (1 Cor 13), that it is righteousness, peace, and joy in the Holy Spirit (Rom 14:17) ... and that its characteristic acts (Rom 12:10-21) are typically impossible without Holy Spirit empowerment (Gal 5:16-26). (Cox, 2011)

We want to invite the Holy Spirit to take over our teaching, to break into our lessons, to change lives supernaturally. Only as we allow Him to have His way will we experience Kingdom education.

Much of what I shared in this chapter came from the research of Dr. William F. Cox, Jr., the founder of the Christian School Program at Regent University. He has spent a lifetime studying and researching best practices in Christian education. He has discovered many key concepts regarding the Kingdom of God. I will rely heavily on his teachings as we have worked closely to develop Kingdom-rich curriculum over the past several years. I also have the privilege of teaching as an adjunct professor at Regent University, and one course I teach is Kingdom Curriculum and Instruction. Many of the quotes throughout this document will come from that material.

THE KINGDOM VIEW OF THE CHILD

The Bible places a high value on children. God created man in His image and gave him dominion over the earth He created (Gen 1:26). In Deuteronomy God commands the parents to train their children in His ways throughout the day (Deut 6:7). God chose Abraham because He knew he would raise his children in the ways of God. Genesis 18:19 says, "For I have chosen him, so that he will direct his children and his household after him to keep the way of the Lord by doing what is right and just." God gives the charge of children to the parents and it is their responsibility to train them in the ways of the Lord. Proverbs 22:6 says, "Train up a child in the way he should go. And when he is old he will not depart from it." Ephesians 6:4 continues this theme and mentions fathers in particular as responsible for this training, "And you, fathers, do not provoke your children to wrath, but bring them up in the training and admonition of the Lord." Training the next generation in the ways of the Lord is a high and holy calling and a large responsibility, but God gives us the body of Christ, the Holy Spirit, and all we need to do the task He has called us to do.

Jesus had a remarkable view of children and esteemed them as the

> "greatest in the kingdom of God" (Matt18:1-5). He loved them and interacted with them by holding them in His arms, blessing them and healing them. He left for us a model to emulate. (Youmans, 2001-2016)

In Matthew 18:1-5, he taught that a child is the greatest in the Kingdom of heaven. He warned about causing a little one to stumble (Matt 18:6) and said, "Whoever welcomes one such child in my name welcomes me" (Matt 18:5). From this, we can see that Jesus has a very high view of children and teaches us to value them as equal members in His Kingdom.

It is important for parents and teachers to help each child know God has a plan for their life. Here are just a few Scriptures to support this: Jeremiah 1:5 says, "Before I formed you in the womb, I knew you, and before you were born, I consecrated you." The Psalmist David wrote,

> Your eyes have seen my unformed substance; and in Your book were all written the days that were ordained for me, when as yet there was not one of them. How precious also are Your thoughts to me, O God! How vast is the sum of them! (Ps 139: 16-17)

The Apostle Paul wrote," But when God, who had set me apart even from my mother's womb and called me through His grace, was pleased to reveal His Son in me so that I might preach Him among the Gentiles" (Gal 1:15-16). We have a God-given responsibility to help each child know God loves them unconditionally and knows their steps. Jeremiah 29:11 says, "For I know the thoughts that I think toward you, says the Lord, thoughts of peace and not of evil, to give you a future and a hope." We have a high and holy calling to nurture each child in God's kingdom principles so they can be prepared for whatever life calling God has for them.

Why is it so important to have a correct view of children? Our view will dictate how we treat the children in our care. Each society has a view of children. I remember as a child, the old adage was "children should be seen and not heard." We were taught to stop whatever we were doing when my father walked in the door. We would eat together as a family and the children just sat quietly and listened to the adults talk about their day. No one asked us what we learned or how we felt. Now, in America and around the world, we have gone to the other extreme and elevated children to demigods. They rule the home. We schedule our lives around their priorities and many families cannot attend church due to baseball, soccer, football games, etc. We have created a narcissistic society where people take selfies more than admire the amazing world God has created. A proper perspective on childhood is necessary to lay the foundation for Kingdom education.

Your view of children will dictate the kind of education you provide. As Kingdom educators, we believe each child is made in the image of God (Gen 1:26) and, therefore, has the ability to think, reason, worship, create, plan, evaluate their actions, etc. We will explore this further as we discuss the key Kingdom concepts in later chapters. As children made in God's image, each child deserves unconditional love. We emphasize loving relationships, first with God, then others, and, finally, ourselves as image bearers. We also are realistic in our assessment of our children. We believe they are all sinners in need of a savior (Rom 3:23). We teach them about the kingdom of God and the kingdoms of this world and help them to do spiritual warfare through prayer, fasting, etc. We teach the whole child. Our philosophy of education is dependent on the biblical view of children and will be discussed further in the next chapter.

Many of the ideas shared in this chapter came from the foundational work of Dr. Elizabeth Youmans, founder of Chrysalis International, Inc. (www.amoprogram.com) and Dr. Carole Adams, founder of Stonebridge School and President of the Foundation for American Christian Education (www.face.net). I had the privilege of working closely with these two mighty women of God when I taught at Stonebridge School in Chesapeake, Virginia. They trained me in the Principle Approach®, which is a biblical historical method of education I highly recommend. If you are interested in further training, they both have intensive training available. Dr. Youmans trains international leaders in these life-giving principles through her Apprenticeship Program and Dr. Adams trains Principle Approach® teachers. You can explore both by using the links I provided. The purpose of this chapter was to give you a brief overview of the key ideas about educating children from a Biblical, Christian perspective.

PHILOSOPHY OF KINGDOM EDUCATION

In Webster's 1828 American Dictionary of the English Language, he defines philosophy as

> a noun [Latin *philosophia;* Gr. *love, to love, and wisdom.*]. Literally, the love of wisdom. ... an explanation of the reasons of things; or an investigation of the causes of all phenomena both of mind and of matter. When applied to any particular department of knowledge, it denotes the collection of general laws or principles under which all the subordinate phenomena or facts relating to that subject, are comprehended...The objects of *philosophy* are to ascertain facts or truth, and the causes of things or their phenomena; to enlarge our views of God and his works, and to render our knowledge of both practically useful and subservient to human happiness.

True religion and true philosophy must ultimately arrive at the same principle. Thus, philosophy is the underlying love of wisdom and encompasses all we teach. It lays the foundation for what we teach and how we teach it. Everything we teach relates to God and His Kingdom.

I love the way Hillsdale College defines philosophy too.

> The original meaning of philosophy (*philo-sophia*), 'the love of wisdom.' As *love*, philosophy is motivated by a felt need or desire, what Aristotle called "wonder:" "For it is owing to their wonder that men both now begin and first began to philosophize" (*Metaphysics* I.2). Wonder desires to know the causes of things, not for the sake of some useful purpose, but simply because such knowledge is regarded as good in itself. (Hillsdale College, n.d.)

They conclude the following, "the philosophical quest for Wisdom inevitably becomes a search for God. Philosophy always leads to theology."

We cannot separate our philosophy from our quest to know God better. As we fall deeper in love with God, we have a desire to know more about the world He created and "study to show ourselves approved unto God, a workman that needs not be ashamed, rightly dividing the Word of truth" (II Tim 2:15). The Bible itself does warn us about vain philosophies in Colossians 2:8 "Beware lest any man spoil you through philosophy and vain deceit, after the traditions of men, after the rudiments of the world and not after Christ." Every form of education has a philosophy which will fundamentally lead students either into a deeper walk with God or away from Him. Our goal as Kingdom educators is to bring our students face-to-face with the living God every day in every subject we teach.

Let's take a closer look at some common philosophies of education and their end products. A chart comparing these two views of education is part of the AMO training and may be available through contacting Dr. Elizabeth Youmans (www.amoprogram.com) and is based on the work of the Foundation for American Christian Education by the late Rosalie Slater. The traditional view of education sees the child as a blank slate, clay in the hands of the teacher and parents to be molded and shaped as they see fit. The goal of education is to modify their behavior to conform with the needs of society. The spirit of learning is dependent on the teacher. They hold the answers to all the questions. A teacher's directed instruction has to be common to all equally. It has a consumer mentality of learning with workbooks that are used up and gotten through each year to be discarded and started again with a major review in the new school year. Teachers assume the students are empty vessels that need refilling as the facts seem to keep leaking out. The methods used appeal to the external. Teachers have a balancing act between entertaining the students to keep them engaged and controlling their behavior and waning attention. Since learning is not authentic, it tends to be boring, so students constantly need to switch from one topic to another to help keep their attention. The curriculum is taught piecemeal, which means nothing is seen as connected to the other subjects, so math is distinct from history or writing. It must be dumbed down so the average child can get it, which leaves the bright students to teach themselves, get in trouble, or be bored. It also leaves the slower learners behind, since they cannot attain the mastery of these most basic ideas. The teacher's job is an impossible situation, but it is justified in that they "get through the curriculum." They are not required to actually teach the students given to their charge, but only take them through the year and they will pass on to the next teacher, who will continue the same process. The results are socialization of the child, training them to be dependent on others. It does not produce a child who can think and reason independently but one who relies on social media to set the standards for right and wrong. Whatever is popular is right. There are no fixed standards of morality or right and wrong. It teaches situational ethics. It also values tolerance above truth. All religions are seen equally as valid. Every myth about creation is equal to the truth in God's Word or, perhaps, of higher value, since they do not claim to be the only truth as Jesus did.

In contrast to this, we have transformational education. We will refer to this as biblical or Kingdom education. The view of the child is foundational to this philosophy of education. We believe humans are made in the image of God (Gen 1:26). This means each individual is full, creative, and gifted. The goal is a transformed heart. It is all about relationships. First, a loving relationship with God and then with others. Each year, we start with the sovereignty of God and introduce our students to the God of the universe who reigns and is intimately acquainted with each one of us. The spirit of learning is independent, productive, and creative. We want students to become masters of their subjects by going deeply into the creation in order to have dominion over the earth. Our method is to appeal to the internal from cause to effect. We delve deeply into the subjects. We inspire and consecrate our students to be lifelong lovers of learning. We give them the tools to be independent learners. We rejoice when they come to class and share what they are learning outside of the classroom. We celebrate learning as part of our curriculum, which includes special days when we focus on the contributions of others and add to their body of learning. The curriculum is elevated, whole, and taught by principles. The results are astounding. We are seeking the attainment of the child's full potential in Christ.

DO ACADEMIC RESULTS MATTER?

The idea of academics and their value is a controversial issue. On one hand, as a school, we are responsible to focus on academics. On the other hand, we are training disciples to rule and reign with Christ, and our emphasis should be on eternal things. Some people see these two ideas as antithetical, but I believe we need a balance. We need to be true to our mission and educate children in academics, but our highest goal should be preparing them for eternity with God. I do not believe it is an either/or proposition. I believe we use academics as the tool to bring children into a loving relationship with God. We want them to see that God is sovereign over everything. As St. Augustine taught that all truth is God's truth.

How do we balance academics with teaching Kingdom principles? First, I would recommend starting every year with a focus on the sovereignty of God. We need to introduce our students to the living God who created everything out of nothing (Gen 1). Webster's 1828 defines *sovereign* as, "1. Supreme in power; possessing supreme dominion; as a *sovereign* ruler of the universe. 2. Supreme; superior to all others; chief. God is the *sovereign* good of all who love and obey him." God is sovereign over everything. There are three main reasons we explain to children that God is sovereign. First, He is sovereign because He is the only God and, therefore, has the right to rule everything. Second, God is sovereign because He created everything; therefore, He has the right to rule His creation. Third, God is just. He is both loving and just; therefore, He sets the standards for right and wrong (Hayford, 1995). As we bring children into a loving relationship with God, they will be prepared to study about His creation and understand their rightful place in God's kingdom. We recommend teaching these concepts through opening exercises, during daily devotional times within the classrooms, and as they come up in academics. For instance, when you teach science, start with the story of creation in Genesis 1. When you teach history, share how God intervenes in the affairs of men and nations. When teaching math, show how numbers are infinite, which is a reflection of God's character. No matter what number you think of you can always add more to it. This is just a brief introduction, but we will discuss how to do this more thoroughly with every subject later on in the book.

Once we introduce the sovereignty of God, we want to focus on the biblical charges God has given us. If God is sovereign, He has the right to tell us what He expects from us. The first is to love God with all your heart, soul, mind, and strength (Deut 6:5). "And the second is like it: 'You shall love your neighbor as yourself.'" (Matt 22:39; Lev 19:18). This biblical charge also assumes you love yourself, so we focus on teaching students who they are as made in the image of God. Other biblical charges will be covered in the curriculum and we will introduce them throughout the year. They include "Be holy for I am holy" (Lev 11:45); the great commission to "Go into all the world and preach the gospel to every creature" (Mark 16:15); and the Dominion Mandate.

Once students understand who God is, the next logical step is to introduce how we are made in the image of God. We refer to this as God's principle of individuality or the imago Dei authentication. Genesis 1:26 says,

> Then God said, "Let Us make man in Our image, according to Our likeness; let them have dominion over the fish of the sea, over the birds of the air, and over the cattle, over all the earth and over every creeping thing that creeps on the earth."

We will refer to this as the Dominion Mandate. Man was created in the image of God and given dominion over creation. We study academics in order to fulfill this biblical charge.

All academics are necessary to help us better understand the principles of the universe and how things work in God's created order. When we study math, science, health, history, geography, etc., we are taking dominion over those subjects. We believe each subject should be taught whole and complete. We teach students the principles behind the subjects, not just random facts. By teaching in this way, we are fulfilling our high calling and preparing students to be masters of the subjects, not just to get into a good school or college, but to be prepared to think and reason biblically from cause to effect. Understanding who we are and the value God puts on the individual is critical in the body of Christ. People who do not see their own worth are more prone to mental disorders and to be deceived by the enemy. We teach every child their value to God. He loves us so much that He made us in His image. He gave us the power to love, to reason, to create, to imagine, etc. We also teach that no two individuals are alike. That is part of God's wonderful design. He creates each one unique with special gifts and talents that they contribute to the body of Christ. Each person is of inestimable value! This principle can be readily taught using academics. For instance, in science, you can study rocks, leaves, seashells, snowflakes, fruit, fingerprints, etc. Each one is unique and shows God's infinite creativity. Not even identical twins are identical. They have different personalities and potential. We see this principle in mathematics too. Every number is unique from all others. The number 3 is different from 5 or 7. We study key individuals in history and literature, identifying their contributions and backgrounds and how God used them as a part of His master plan. So, you see, we do teach these principles through the academic subjects; thus, academics do matter, but they are subservient to the fundamental principles of the Kingdom we are teaching. We also teach these principle during our Bible classes, devotional times, and our group assemblies.

Along with God's principle of individuality, we also teach the kingdom concept of identity and destiny affirmation. Both believers and nonbelievers have value because God made us in His image (Imago Dei), and since God was willing to send His only son Jesus to die for us when we were yet sinners (Rom 5:8). We want to help our children understand how valuable they are through teaching them they are part of Christ's body on earth (Eph 4:25), they are His children (John 1:12), heirs with Christ (Gal 4:7), and the temple of the Holy Spirit (1 Cor 6:19) (Cox, 2016). As students understand their identity in the body of Christ, they will understand God has an amazing destiny for them that only they can fulfil. We do this daily through affirming the children as they share their ideas in class discussions. We treat them as full and complete, not empty vessels needing to be filled. We ask them higher-level reasoning questions and expect them to be able to reason biblically from an early age. By setting high expectations, we are training children in the way they should go (Proverbs 22:6).

Once the children understand who they are in Christ and the incredible value God places on the individual, it is time to teach them the principle of unity out of our diversity along with life in the body of Christ. We are all unique creations of God and should value that in each other. We need each person in the body of Christ (Rom 12:4, 5, 10). The weaker parts need the most protection (1 Cor 12). If we truly love God, we will also love those who are made in His image. We will love one another and esteem each other better than ourselves (Phil 2:3). How do we teach this through academics? We study key individuals and talk about their contribution to the forward movement of the gospel. Whenever we study science, we talk about the contributions of key scientists and how they used their gifts to benefit mankind. In history, we study key individuals and share how God used them to benefit all mankind. We study the good examples and those who are not models of Christian character and help the students see how our life choices are not our own but affect others as well. When a student is sharing an answer in class, we train our students to listen attentively and learn from one another.

This leads us to the principle of Christian Self-Government. In the garden of Eden, God gave Adam and Eve the tree of the knowledge of good and evil to test them. They failed the test and sin entered the world. Yet, without the tree, humans would not have had free will. God wants us to love Him because we choose to do so, not out of coercion. The gift of free will is an amazing gift God has given us. We teach children they have the ability to choose to serve God or serve self. We teach them about God's kingdom and the kingdom of Satan. These principles are taught in academics as we study the influence of men and women and how they either chose to follow God's way or walk in their own ways. We emphasize Christian self-government and help the students realize they cannot govern themselves apart from Christ; they need to submit to the Lordship of Christ daily in order to please Him (Gal 5:22-25).

This leads naturally to the kingdom principle of Holy Spirit Empowerment. We cannot live the Christian life without the help of the Holy Spirit. Jesus said it was more beneficial for Him to go away so He could send us the Holy Spirit to help us and lead us into all truth (John 15:26; 16:13). Ephesians 5:15-20 teaches us to be careful how we live and to be filled with the Spirit. The book of Acts is full of examples of the Holy Spirit intervening, directing, healing, empowering, etc. As the body of Christ, we have the same power the early Christians and Apostles had. We are to manifest the power of the Holy Spirit every day in our academic pursuits. We begin classes by stopping and inviting the Holy Spirit to break into our prepared lessons and be the teacher. We teach our students to pray personally and ask the Holy Spirit to enlighten them when they don't understand something. James 1:5 says, "If any of you lacks wisdom, let him ask of

God, who gives to all liberally, and without reproach, and it will be given him. (NKJV)" God invites us to ask Him for help in our academics and He is faithful to empower us. I have many examples of teaching and finding the students just were not getting it, then I would stop and pray and, instantly, understanding would come. Sometimes, He would show me a new way of explaining it and, other times, a student would give the light that was needed, and we would rejoice together.

Other principles and Kingdom keys will be discussed later, but these were given so you would have an idea of how we will use the principles and Kingdom concepts to strengthen the study of academics. They are not taught separately, but are part of our academic studies. We are called to have dominion over the earth, and part of that charge is to master academics. God is pleased when we ask Him to help us be better teachers and students, just as He was when Solomon asked for wisdom to guide his people (I Kings 3 & 4). Ask boldly and trust God to lead you into all truth.

BIBLICAL METHODOLOGY

Deuteronomy 6 is the foundation for the biblical methodology we are proposing. First, it is a divinely relational methodology. It is based on loving God first and foremost and obeying His commands. Second, it is humanly relational, as it is primarily done within the family relationship. The parents are to transfer the fear of the Lord to their children by demonstrating a loving relationship with God and instructing and impressing these laws on their own children. The fear of the Lord is demonstrated as parents reverence God by putting Him first in all they do, honoring Him with their time and talents, and keeping His commandments. Parents are the first teachers. We are admonished to teach the next generation to observe God's commands. That is to teach them to obey God and follow His commands diligently. Our primary responsibility is to transfer the fear of the Lord to the children we are entrusted with. We are to focus on creating a loving relationship with our students by demonstrating how much God loves us and how we live in loving obedience to God. Each year, we need to focus on introducing our students to God. Children who get to know God personally are less likely to leave the faith according to Barna (2003).

How do we teach them to observe the commands of the Lord? We begin each day with a time of daily devotions. We give students the opportunity to get to know God through His Word, prayer, praise, and worship. We spend time with God daily and make it a priority in our schedules. Adding a chapel once a week is good and necessary, but it shouldn't replace the time of daily waiting on the Lord and hearing His voice. Make time so students can bring their prayer requests before God and keep track of His amazing answers to prayer.

"The fear of the Lord is the beginning of knowledge, but fools despise wisdom and instruction" (Proverbs 1:7). The Lord is sovereign of the Universe. He is the ruler of all creation because He made it out of nothing and, therefore, has the right to rule it. He is also the sovereign because He is the one and only God. He also is totally good and because He is holy, He deserves our worship. We need to introduce our students to the sovereign God and teach them to stand in awe of His majesty. One way to do that is to study the names of God and what they teach us about His character. You could create a bulletin board and set aside a place in the room where students could add names of God as they discover them in their reading of the Bible collectively and individually.

Throughout the Deuteronomy 6 passage, we see the connection between hearing and keeping all His commands and decrees. It is imperative that students not only learn the commands of the Lord but also fully obey them. Hearing and obeying are linked together. Some ideas for this would be to have a copy of the Ten Commandments on the wall of your classroom or home. Refer to these foundational laws and teach how they are the basis for civil government. The first commandments are directed toward loving God and obeying Him. The second half of the commandments have to do with loving our neighbor as ourselves. Jesus quoted Deuteronomy 6 when answering the Pharisees about the greatest commandment.

> Jesus replied: "'Love the Lord your God with all your heart and with all your soul and with all your mind.' This is the first and greatest

> commandment. And the second is like it: 'Love your neighbor as yourself.' All the Law and the Prophets hang on these two commandments" (Matt 22:37-40).

Our classroom rules should be a reflection of these as well. If we bring our children into right relationship with God early, they will want to honor the image of God in their fellow students. The closer we walk in the laws of God, the easier the discipline of our students becomes, since Jesus is the standard and He gives us the power to do right as we submit our wills to His.

How can we impress them on our children? The secret is we need to focus on God and His kingdom throughout the day in every subject we teach. We need to be sure every subject is taught from a biblical perspective. From Deuteronomy 6, we need to talk about them "when you sit at home and when you walk along the road." It needs to be like breathing, it is so natural to us. We need to ask God for our daily needs and praise Him when He comes through and provides for us. We need to sing songs of worship and praise throughout the day and impress them on the hearts of our children. In every situation, it is appropriate to talk about the things of the Lord. Recently, my grandson wanted something from Target and was saving up to get it, but only one was left. He was concerned it wouldn't still be there when we went to pick it up after he got his allowance later in the week, so I told him to pray about it. He prayed a sweet prayer of faith, and when we got there on Friday, there was not just one but three of his item. His little sister yelled, "Hallelujah Holy Spirit!" We laughed together and shared that God the Father, God the Son, and God the Holy Spirit all heard and answered his prayer. Moments like these are the norm for children who are being impressed with God's closeness and care about every detail of their lives.

The next reference in Deuteronomy 6 is to talk about them "When you lie down and when you get up." As parents, grandparents, caregivers, or teachers, it should be the most natural thing to thank God for a new day and to rejoice in His provision at the end of the day. We say our prayers nightly with our children and should tuck them into bed with the love of the Lord on their hearts and minds. When they have bad dreams, we teach them Scripture, like "perfect love casts out all fear." My grandchildren say, "fear, fear get out of here in the name of Jesus." They know to take authority over their thoughts and to bring each one captive to the obedience of Christ (2 Cor. 10:5).

"Tie them as symbols on your hands and bind them on your foreheads." We don't literally wear the Scriptures today, but we can memorize them. This assures we will have them close at hand to use as the Holy Spirit directs us. Children are very adept at memorizing. The Scriptures they memorize as children serve them well for a lifetime. A great way to memorize the Word is through Scripture songs. Songs go into a long-term storage in the brain and can be recalled much easier than just memorizing random verses. Another great way to memorize the Word is to concentrate on longer passages, rather than isolated verses. When we learn something in context, it stays with us longer. For instance, choose a passage of scripture like Romans 12 and memorize it as a whole school or family.

The last part of the Deuteronomy 6 passage says to "write them." That leads directly into the formal method we use to teach our students. It is known as the notebook method and is a biblical method of learning. We have the Word of God in our own language because someone who came before us was diligent to write down the Scriptures. In the Old Testament, each king was required to write out the law for himself so that he could govern according to God's precepts (Deut 17:18). Writing teaches discipline and helps children focus on the Word of God.

The Notebook Method

The notebook method was developed as a tool for reflective learning in the Principle Approach, as developed by Rosalie Slater at the Foundation for American Christian Education.

It employs the four natural or biblical steps of learning, which she termed: **research, reason, relate, and record.** It is an ancient method of study, one used by many of the world's greatest thinkers and writers throughout history. It began when God instructed Moses to write down what He was saying and rehearse it in the ears of Joshua (Exod 17:14). God has always placed great value on the written word.

This educational tool guides reflection and deductive reasoning by principles. It introduces both the teacher and the student to the study of the subject through the nature and character of God as its Author. It lays the foundation for thinking and reasoning on the light and eternal life of God's Word! It breaks open the subject with its key terms and principles and enlightens the pathway of thinking and reasoning for eventual mastery of the subject. This reflective method requires time and a commitment to excellence. All education produces a specific character. The notebook method produces Christian character and scholarship.

Research To diligently inquire and examine in seeking facts and principles (Ezra 6:1-2; John 5:39; Acts 17:11). Examples: Performing biblical word studies by researching the vocabulary used and the biblical foundation of the subject to reveal the nature and character of God in the subject; Researching from primary sources; Gathering facts, rules, definitions, maps, charts, etc.

Reason To identify the cause or ground of conclusion; that which supports or justifies (Ps 119: 169; Isa 1:18; Acts 17:2; 19:9; 1 Cor 13:11). Examples: Deducing principles from God's Word which produce moral rectitude; Outlining the subject; Performing assignments requiring reasoning from cause to effect in essay format which produces abstract and critical thinking skills that eventually lead to original thought and idea

Relate To tell or recite; to apply fact and truth to life and knowledge (Mark 9:9; Luke 24:35; Acts 21:19). Examples: Writing definitions and deduced principles in your own words; Writing out lessons learned and relating them to your own life; Solving problems; Performing

> experiments; Taking tests; Writing essays, speeches, thesis, oratories, dramas, musicals; Orally defending thesis
>
> **Record** To write an authentic copy for preservation of what was taught or studied (Exod 17:14; Deut 17:18-20; Ezra 4:15; Hab 2:2; Mal 3:16-18; Matt 1:1; Luke 10:20). Examples: Student's notebook work, essays, compositions, and poems; Journals; Personal and public correspondence; Delivering speeches and oratories; Debates; Paintings; Dramatic and musical performances; Thesis and defending one's thesis. (Youmans, 2001-2016)

This methodology has produced some of the world's greatest thinkers and leaders to date and it will be effective no matter what teaching situation you find yourself in. If you are a homeschooling Mother or a Christian or public school teacher, you can begin by having your child learn the writing cycle. Start with a sentence and teach the grammatical components. Then build to a paragraph and from that to a three-paragraph essay. As they master the writing process you can teach various kinds of paragraphs and work up to a research paper. Sir Francis Bacon, the English Essayist said, "Reading makes a man full. Speaking – a ready man. Writing makes him exact." Our goal is to polish the student's ability to communicate so they can share the gospel in words and other creative ways.

Teaching by Principles

The methodology we use in Kingdom education is based on teaching by principles. Principles are leading ideas that guide our studies. Webster's 1828 *American Dictionary of the English Language* defines a *principle* as,

> In a general sense, the cause, source or origin of anything; that from which a thing proceeds; as the principle of motion; the principles of action... A general truth; a law comprehending many subordinate truths; as the principles of morality, of law, of government, etc.

There are many different kinds of principles and we will discuss a few of them briefly. This is not an exhaustive list, but rather a sampling. Please feel free to add other principles that you discover in your personal studies.

Biblical Principles

As many biblical principles exist, this is just a sample to give you the general idea. The Bible begins with the creation story. In it, we see a governmental principle. God says, "Let there be light" and there was light, and God saw that it was good. The idea of I plan, I do, I judge is a governmental principle that can be deduced from this example and is seen throughout Scripture. God gives Gideon the battle plan, he executes the plan, then he judges how successful it was accomplished. This is an example of a biblical principle. Another one is "What you sow you will also reap" (Gal 6:7,8). "Do onto others as you would have them do unto you," (Luke 6:31). The idea of biblical principles is that they teach us what God's Kingdom is like and how to live in the Kingdom. These are not a list of rules, but rather overarching principles that we use to further develop our curriculum and teaching.

Kingdom Principles

Kingdom principles are deduced from the teachings of Christ in the New Testament, particularly the Gospels, but also the other New Testament writers who interpreted the principles and further applied them to life. An example of a Kingdom Principle is "Be merciful, for your Father also is merciful" (Luke 6:36). Many other Kingdom principles are part of the Sermon on the Mount found in Matthew 5-7. "Judge not, that ye be not judged" (Matt 7:1). These principles lead to living in the Kingdom, which is contrary to the way the world generally works. God's Kingdom is counterintuitive. In our flesh, we want to promote ourselves, rise to the top of the heap, push down others along the way, but Jesus teaches us the first shall be last. If the world praises and approves of us, then we have our reward already. He teaches us to put others' needs before our own. These Kingdom principles will be the basis for our curriculum.

Seven Governmental Principles of the Principle Approach

Rosalie Slater, the educator, and Verna Hall, the historian, examined the Scriptures for a biblical method of education. They developed the Principle Approach which is based on the American Christian form of government. These governmental principles are based on Scripture, but they are also governmental principles. I will state them briefly here, but not go into detail, as they are primarily governmental principles. They are very powerful and will transform your classroom if you apply them. For more detailed information about these principles, visit the Foundation for American Christian Education (www.-face.net/the-seven-principles/). They are: 1. God's Principle of Individuality, 2. The Principle of Christian Self-Government, 3. The Principle of Christian Character, 4. Conscience is the Most Sacred Property, 5. The Christian Form of our Government, 6. Planting the Seed of Local Self-Government, and 7. American Political Union. In the next chapter, I will demonstrate how you can use these principles in Kingdom education.

Subject Principles

The last kind of principle we will examine here is a subject principle. Each subject has overarching truths that guide the teaching of that subject. For instance, "What you sow you will also reap" is a biblical principle but also a foundational principle in the study of botany. If you plant corn seeds, you will not reap watermelon. This principle is necessary for the survival of our species. If we planted seeds and something random came up every time, we might starve to death while waiting for an edible crop. Instead God set this principle in motion in Genesis when he said every plant would bear seeds "after its own kind." This assures us that a loving Father is watching over us and is supplying all our needs. In mathematics, we use principles such as the Commutative Property of Addition, which says 2 + 3 = 3 + 2. We can change the order of the addends without changing the quantity. In history, we might study the idea of how "Power corrupts, and absolute power corrupts absolutely." We use subject principles in every subject we teach. These are just a few examples to help you start thinking about subject principles. One way to discover the most important subject principles is to go to the library and get a children's book on that subject. For instance, a book on physics from a children's library would list the key principles of that subject and can greatly assist you when beginning your study of a new subject. More about this in our next chapter.

Hebrew vs. Greek Model

Before we move away from the topic of methodology, we need to review that every philosophy of education produces a product. In America and most of the world, we rely on the Greek model of educating. We teach by separate subjects, piecemeal. The goal is to produce educated students who have covered a variety of subjects and have a basic familiarity with them. The Hebrew model of education was much different. It taught subjects holistically. It was not divided into separate subjects as the Greek model. The goal of a Hebrew education was a relationship with the Almighty God. Children memorized large portions and whole books of the Torah. The main emphasis was obedience and trust in God (Edelmann, 2006). Kingdom methodology will be following this Hebrew model more closely. The goal is one of building a loving relationship, first with God and then with others. Children are made in the image of God and are complete in Him. We will be focusing on going deeply into subjects as a means of strengthening our relationship with God, self, and others.

HOW TO DEVELOP CURRICULUM

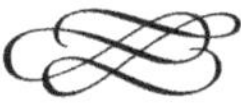

We have already looked at the methodology we use in Kingdom education. So, now, we will look at how to develop your curriculum. Unfortunately, no solid Kingdom education curriculum is available; therefore, you will need to develop your own. This is both a challenge and an awesome responsibility. As you set out to help further the kingdom in your life and that of your students, you will be partnering with the Holy Spirit. God's Word assures us that the Holy Spirit will guide us into all truth (John 16:13). So, the first step in developing your curriculum is to **pray and seek the Lord**. Ask God for wisdom and He promises in His word to give it to you (James 1:5).

Study God's Word

The next step is to **study God's Word** for yourself. Read it, study it, and meditate on it. As you do this, you will begin to notice themes or principles that recur. A good beginning might be to start by reading through the gospels and making a list of the teachings of Jesus. What themes did he speak of often? How did He describe the Kingdom of

God? What did He say about the Kingdom of Heaven? How are these two related?

There are many great tools to help you in Bible study. One I strongly recommend is called the Blue Letter Bible. It is free to download at blueletterbible.org. When you read a passage, you can double click on it and it opens up Bible dictionaries, concordances, cross-references, and many other study tools.

Another great tool is Bible Gateway (biblegateway.com). This is a tool for looking up key words or phrases and getting other references. For instance, try looking up the word *Kingdom, Kingdom of God,* or *Kingdom of Heaven.* You can print out a list of these references and begin a personal study of what the Bible says about this topic. (See a copy in Chapter Twelve.)

Also, study Bibles and many other tools are available for you to use in your study, but don't get bogged down in what other people have said about a topic; study it for yourself. The Holy Spirit is the great teacher and He will guide and direct you. Ask Him for His help and thank Him when He shows you things (1 Cor 2:13) be sure to record them in a notebook or on your computer.

Derive Biblical Principles

Principles are derived from studying and meditating on God's Word. The Holy Spirit will lead you to biblical truths that occur more than once in Scripture. These are the truths you want to use to further develop your curriculum. They are the overarching themes or big ideas. An example of one would be, "If you want to be great in God's Kingdom, learn to be the servant of all" (Matt 23:11). This idea is contrary to the way the world works. In society, the greatest people have servants to wait on them. In God's Kingdom, the greatest become the servants of all. Jesus demonstrated this when He washed His disciples' feet at the last supper (John 13). The woman who had been forgiven much washed Jesus's feet and dried them with her hair (Luke 7). Jesus tells us whatever we do for the least of these His children, we do it unto Him (Matt 25:40). We are called to serve others.

This principle can be taught and applied in every subject. In the Bible, it is clearly taught. Even in the Old Testament, we see many examples of this. For instance, Ruth was a great example of a servant as she went out daily to glean in the fields and share what she gathered with her mother-in-law Naomi. Joseph served in the prison faithfully before he was chosen to be second in command to the Pharaoh. Rebekah was chosen because she was willing to draw water for the camels (Gen 24). As you study various key individuals in Scripture, point out this Kingdom principle.

You can apply it in literature by looking for examples of characters who demonstrate this trait. In the book, *The Lion, The Witch, and the Wardrobe* by C.S. Lewis, you can compare and contrast Edmond and Lucy. Edmond did not exhibit this principle in his life in the beginning. He was selfish and conceited and very difficult to live with until he met Aslan, who sacrificed his life to save Edmond. His character changes dramatically at the end of the story and he becomes a true servant leader. Lucy, on the other hand, was kind and selfless right from the start. She truly demonstrated a servant's heart.

You can apply the same principle in math or science by exploring men or women who have put the welfare of others before themselves. For instance, Harriet Tubman and the underground railroad. George Washington Carver who discovered hundreds of uses for the peanut and revolutionized agriculture in the South. He didn't just stay within the walls of the college but would travel around with a cart and demonstrate his principles to local farmers. His life story is an amazing example of this very principle.

Explore Subject Principles

Every subject has principles or leading ideas that are critical to mastering the subject. We often call these objectives and they are located in the overview of the curriculum you are using. If you are developing Kingdom curriculum, you will need to ascertain these key subject principles in order to form overviews and lesson plans. We start with the end in mind. What do you want your students to know about the subject at hand? Let's use botany for an example. What are some of the key ideas to master when studying botany? First, they need to have a basic understanding of the vocabulary of the subject. Some key words might be *botany, biology, plants, species,* etc. We then go to Noah Webster's *1828 American Dictionary of the English Language.* We recommend this dictionary because it goes back to the original languages and it also uses the Bible for the foundation of many definitions, so part of your work is already done for you. I like to use an online version for ease of use while some prefer to have the actual words in front of them. Whichever is most convenient for your situation is best for you. If you do not have a reliable Internet provider, then you need an actual copy of the dictionary. There are several online versions you can use for free if you have Internet connectivity.

Here is the definition for Botany: "Botany is the science of the structure, functions, properties, habits and arrangement of plants, and of the technical characteristics by which they are distinguished." This helps you to devise the subject principles. We need to teach the structure of the plant: roots, stem, leaves, flower, etc. If you are teaching young children, that may be enough, but if you are teaching older students, you would want to break down the structure even further. What are the functions of plants? This leads into leading ideas like food production, oxygen–carbon dioxide transfer, soil erosion, etc.

What are the properties of plants compared to animals? How are they similar and how are they different? Habitats of plants – what kinds of plants grow in the woods, the desert, the ocean, etc.? What does a plant need in order to grow? Where do plants come from? Seeds, cuttings, bulbs, spores, etc. If you are dealing with older students you might want to bring in the whole idea of Latin classification and taxonomy. You see how by looking up one word, you have begun to develop a rich curriculum that can be customized to your specific needs. Continue this process looking up each key word and recording what you are learning in a notebook or on your computer. These definitions will be a critical part of your lesson plans.

Another excellent source to help you get started with a new topic of study is to go to the children's section of the library and refer to children's books on your topic. They have synthesized the most important information on the topic. It may help you to discover something you didn't already think about in your initial study of the topic. They also have experiments and hands-on activities that will enrich the learning.

Enrichment Ideas

As we set out to develop Kingdom curriculum, we need to start with the foundation of the Word of God, define our terms, synthesize the key principles of the subject, and then look for ways to make the subject come alive for our students. As you the teacher become excited about learning, you will share that love of learning with your students. Look for ways to make the learning practical and applicable for your situation.

Bringing art into the study of the subject is a way to enhance the learning. For instance, even young children can draw diagrams to demonstrate the parts of a plant for instance. Then look for famous art work that depicts pictures of plants. If you have access to the Internet, you can do a Google search. If not, go to a local library and check out some art books and bring them into the classroom. Calendars and old magazines are an inexpensive way to bring classical art into the classroom to enrich your study. The resources are there, we just need to try to get them for our students to enjoy. Van Gogh's "Still Life: Vase with Fourteen Sunflowers" is one example of the beauty of plants in art (https://commons.wikimedia.org/wiki/File:Vincent_Willem_van_Gogh_ 127.jpg).

Another avenue for enriching the curriculum is through poetry. Here is a classic example:

I Wandered Lonely as a Cloud
by William Wordsworth
from www.poetryfoundation.org

I wandered lonely as a cloud
That floats on high o'er vales and hills,
When all at once I saw a crowd,
A host, of golden daffodils;
Beside the lake, beneath the trees,
Fluttering and dancing in the breeze.

Continuous as the stars that shine
And twinkle on the milky way,
They stretched in never-ending line
Along the margin of a bay:
Ten thousand saw I at a glance,
Tossing their heads in sprightly dance.

The waves beside them danced; but they
Out-did the sparkling waves in glee:
A poet could not but be gay,
In such a jocund company:
I gazed—and gazed—but little thought
What wealth the show to me had brought:

For oft, when on my couch I lie
In vacant or in pensive mood,
They flash upon that inward eye
Which is the bliss of solitude;

And then my heart with pleasure fills,
And dances with the daffodils.

You see how enriching art and poetry can be to the study of botany! Read the poem and have your students draw what they see in their mind's eye. Talk about the value of plants that goes beyond food production. Lead them into a discussion of beauty and how God created flowers just for man's pleasure. As we rejoice in God's creation together, we fall deeper in love with our loving Father and Creator, who designs some things simply for the joy they bring us.

Much research has been done about how classical music affects plant growth. "Plants exposed to Hayden, Beethoven, Brahms, and Schubert grew towards and entwined themselves around the speakers" (Mazian, 2019, para. 13). While another group that listened to rock music actually grew away from the speakers. Some plants exposed to a single note actually died. This leads to a fascinating discussion of how music affects us. God's Kingdom is all about worshipping the King with melodies and harmonies, but the kingdom of this world is filled with discordant sounds. Help your students discover how important music is to every living being through exposing them to many varieties of music.

Classic literature is another way to enrich your study. For instance, when we studied botany we also read *The Secret Garden* by Frances Hodgson Burnett. This story is about how a garden helps a little girl who is suffering great loss come alive. It is a lovely story of friendship and healing.

Biographies of famous botanists are also a way to enrich your study and bring in the wholistic aspect of learning. I would recommend reading George Washington Carver's autobiography. He was an amazing man of science and man of God. He loved to worship and he singlehandedly revolutionized agriculture in the South after the American Civil War.

Another important way to enrich the curriculum is through special days. Learning should be celebrated as a whole family. Special days give the students an opportunity to showcase what they have been learning. They display their art, diagrams, notebooks, experiments, etc. They may cook food that they actually grew in their class garden. It is an enriching time of celebration. After each unit study, give the children an opportunity to celebrate what they have learned and how it will enrich the Kingdom of God. This is also a great way to have open houses to promote your school in the community. Invite family and friends as well as people from your local government, newspaper reporters, etc. Kingdom education is radically different from what is going on in the secular schools, and by demonstrating the richness of your curriculum, you are spreading the good news of the Kingdom with others. Cast your net wide and see what God will do.

Develop Clear Measurable Objectives

In order to plan our curriculum, we need to start with the end in mind. What are we trying to accomplish in this unit or lesson plan? Here is a clear definition of objectives from Regis University: "Educational objectives are specific, measurable statements aligned with state standards that describe desired student behavior at the end of a lesson or unit of study. Effective objectives ensure that teachers and students are focused on these outcomes" (Regis University, 2006). The key is that the objective needs to be clearly stated in behavioral terms. What do you want the student to do, know, believe, etc.? It also needs to align with the standards of your state or school district. There is only so much time in a day, so we need to be sure that our goals are aligned with our overall standards.

An excellent resource for curriculum development is *Steppingstones to Curriculum* by Harro Van Brummelen. If you have the opportunity to purchase it, I strongly recommend it. For now, we will begin with one section called "Nine Steps in Planning Classroom Units" (Van Brummelen, 2002, pp. 171). We will modify it slightly to fit the Kingdom education we are designing.

Step 1. Consider the suitability of a proposed topic.

Step 2. Brainstorm ideas, possibly using a planning chart or web diagram.

Step 3. Formulate your unit focus (e.g., a thematic statement, guiding questions, and intended learning outcomes).

Step 4. Design, balance, and sequence learning activities. Include a motivational introductory activity and a culminating summative one.

Step 5. Review linkages with state or provincial standards and/or curriculum guides, adding or revising learning activities accordingly.

Step 6. Plan a schedule.

Step 7. Select your resources.

Step 8. Plan student assessment. Throughout the unit, consider what evidence will show that you have met your intents.

Step 9. Review the effectiveness of your unit.

Let's continue our example of botany for an elementary classroom and go through the steps so you have an example to follow.

Step 1. Consider the suitability of a proposed topic. Let's consider the topic of botany from a Kingdom perspective. Is this a topic that has kingdom value? Yes, we see in Genesis 1:26

> And God said, Let us make man in our image, after our likeness: and let them have dominion over the fish of the sea, and over the fowl of the air, and over the cattle, and over all the earth, and over every creeping thing that creepeth upon the earth.

God gives man dominion over all the earth. This includes botany.

In Genesis 1:11, 12

And God said, Let the earth bring forth grass, the herb yielding seed, and the fruit tree yielding fruit after his kind, whose seed is in itself, upon the earth: and it was so. And the earth brought forth grass, and herb yielding seed after his kind, and the tree yielding fruit, whose see was in itself, after his kind: and God saw that it was good.

The study of botany is implied in the dominion mandate to subdue the earth. Mankind cannot "subdue" what it doesn't understand; therefore, the study of botany is an integral part of the charge God gave mankind in Genesis.

Step 2. Brainstorm ideas, possibly using a planning chart or web diagram.

Whenever you begin a new unit of study, it is important to pray and study God's Word as stated above, then we need to get down to the actual design of the curriculum. One way I like to do that is through brainstorming and creating a mind map. Take a blank sheet of paper and give yourself a set time. Usually ten to fifteen minutes is enough time to begin. Shut out all distractions and begin to write everything you can think about the topic. Remember, you are not planning specific things at this level, just writing everything that comes to mind when you think of botany. Allow your thoughts to run wild and have some fun with it. Here is an example of a mind map for botany.

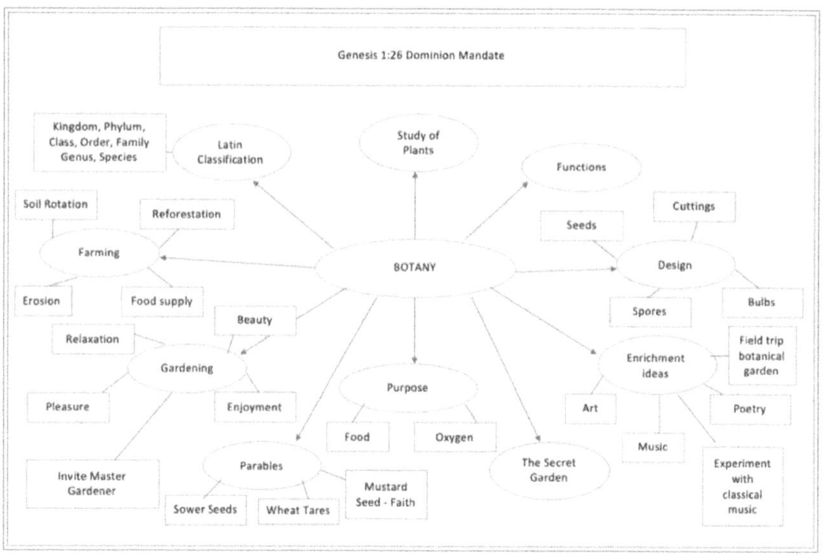

Step 3. Formulate your unit focus (e.g., a thematic statement, guiding questions, and intended learning outcomes). According to Van Brummelen, a thematic statement describes the overall goals that will frame your unit's teaching and learning. "The thematic statement includes the basic values, dispositions, and commitments that you want to foster. The enduring understandings, major concepts, and key skills that you want students to acquire" (Van Brummelen, 2002, p. 180). I like to start with some higher-level thinking questions that begin with "how" and "why" that will frame our exploration. For example, "How do plants help our environment?" "Why do you think God made plants to reproduce after their own kind?" "Imagine what the world would be like without plants. How would life on earth be different?" "What responsibilities do we have for studying botany?" "Why is it worth our time and effort?" This helps lead to my thematic statement: As children of God's kingdom, who have been given dominion over the earth, we need to understand botany to be good stewards of God's creation. This leads to my outcome: The goal of this unit is to help students develop a love and appreciation for the role plants have in sustaining life on earth; to help them fall deeper in love with God as the creator and sustainer of all things; to introduce them to the struc-

ture, functions, properties, habits and arrangement of plants; and to enrich their learning through art, music, literature, and experimentation with plants.

Step 4. Design, balance, and sequence learning activities. Include a motivational introductory activity and a culminating summative one. When planning the actual units of study, it is important to vary the activities to keep learning exciting and meaningful to your students. So much of today's education is simply filling in someone else's blanks. As teachers, we assume the curriculum designers are the experts and we need to blindly follow their plans and sequencing, but this is not true. We are made in the image of God and are creative just as our Father in Heaven is creative. The Holy Spirit came to lead us into all truth. We are equipped by God to guide the students He has entrusted to our care. We can create curriculum that is rich and full and use our students to do it. You do not need to have everything figured out before you begin. Start with what you know and allow the Holy Spirit to guide your decisions. Let the Holy Spirit break into your lesson planning and make your classroom come alive. I have taught this way for many years and find it exciting every day. You make your plans, but God directs your steps. You partner with the God of the universe and create classrooms or true inspirational learning. Our students become lovers of learning and masters of their subjects.

We have already mentioned how we will use art, music, literature, history, writing, etc. Now is the time to decide what activities you will use and in what sequence. In our botany lesson for elementary children, we will include experiments, gardening, drawing diagrams, taking notes, reading, lectures, discussions, and special days. Look at the sample unit overview to see how I might lay out the unit.

Unit Overview

Topic: Botany Genesis 1:11-13

Thematic Statement: As children of God's kingdom, who have been given dominion over the earth, we need to understand botany to be good stewards of God's creation.

Objective: The goal of this unit is to help students develop a love and appreciation for the role plants have in sustaining life on earth; to help them fall deeper in love with God as the creator and sustainer of all things; to introduce them to the structure, functions, properties, habits, and arrangement of plants; to enrich their learning through art, music, literature, and experimentation with plants.

Guiding Questions:

How do plants help our environment?

Why do you think God made plants to reproduce after their own kind?

Imagine what the world would be like without plants.

How would life on earth be different?

What responsibilities do we have for studying botany?

Why is it worth our time and effort?

Linkages with state or provincial standards: (Common Core Curriculum 4th grade Science)

CCSS.ELA-LITERACY.RI.4.2

Determine the main idea of a text and explain how it is supported by key details; summarize the text.

CCSS.ELA-LITERACY.RI.4.9

Integrate information from two texts on the same topic in order to write or speak about the subject knowledgeably.

CCSS.ELA-LITERACY.RI.4.6

Compare and contrast a firsthand and secondhand account of the same event or topic; describe the differences in focus and the information provided.

Resources:

The Bible Genesis 1:11-13

George Washington Carver Biography

Apologia Young Explorer Series: *Exploring Creation with Botany*

Plants, Seeds, Cuttings, Flowers, Microscope, Potting soil, containers, wax paper and iron

Introductory Activity:

Have enough lima beans for each student to have two. Soak them in water overnight. Discuss the importance of a seed to reproduction. Read the Genesis passage about each plant reproducing "after his own kind" and discuss what would happen if seeds didn't reproduce after their own kind. Teach the parts of the seed and have students take notes. Then have them open the seed coat and find the endosperm and embryo.

Student Assessment:

Diagram seed and dissect the lima beans

Reason Questions

Leaf collections

Classification of leaves, seeds, and pictures of various plants

Report on a famous person from Botany

Culminating Activity:

Watch *The Secret Garden* movie. Make a homemade soup with lots of fresh vegetables from a local farmer's market or our school garden. Share with parents and community all the things we have learned about plants. Display notebooks and experiments, art work, etc.

Review the Effectiveness of your unit: Rate each objective on a scale of 1-5, 1 not very effective and 5 very effective.

Did students develop a love and appreciation for God and His creation? 1 2 3 4 5

Did students demonstrate love for God as the creator and sustainer of all things? 1 2 3 4 5

Were students introduced to the structure, functions, properties, habits, and arrangement of plants? 1 2 3 4 5

Were students enriched through art, music, literature, and experimentation with plants? 1 2 3 4 5

Step 5. Review linkages with state or provincial standards and/or curriculum guides, adding or revising learning activities accordingly. Many of you reading this book are working in countries or states that have standards to guide the teaching. Generally, the standards are guidelines that can be adjusted to meet the needs of your particular situation. By aligning our teaching units to specific guidelines and standards, we demonstrate our willingness to follow the standards established. The Bible teaches us to submit to those who are in authority over us (Rom 13). By following the guidelines established, we assure parents that their children are learning what is required as well as going beyond those minimum standards. We are training our students to rule and reign with Christ; therefore, much more is expected of Kingdom education.

Step 6. Plan a schedule. Once you have prepared your unit overview, you want to break the activities down into weekly lesson plans. Generally, in the United States, a school year is divided into four quarters with each one having nine weeks. We will follow that format, but it can be easily adjusted to your specific needs. I will provide blank lesson plans and overview charts in the last chapter. As you make your plans, you will need to adjust it to the number of days you teach the subject and the amount of time you have for each class. If you are homeschooling, you have much more flexibility, so just adjust the plans to fit your needs. I will use a 60-minute teaching schedule twice a week for science class. Generally, I will have a thirty-minute science lesson every day, but sometimes, it is advantageous to spend a longer period on one subject and skip another one, as long as you give enough time to each subject in the overall plan for your year. When starting a new unit, I may take an hour for science and skip history. Then have a longer history lesson later in the week.

Hours	**Monday**	**Tuesday**	**Wednesday**	**Thursday**	**Friday**
8:00-8:10 (10 min.)	Greeting	Greeting	Greeting	Greeting	Greeting
8:10-8:40 (30 min.)	Worship, prayer, praise & Bible story	Worship, prayer, praise & Bible story	Worship, prayer, praise & Bible story	Worship, prayer, praise & Bible story	Worship, prayer, praise & Bible story
8:40-9:20 (40 min.)	Math	Math	Math	Math	Math Games [Assessment]
9:20-9:40 (20 min.)	Snack & Recess	Snack & Recess	Snack & Recess	Snack & Recess	Snack & Recess
9:40-10:40 (60 min.)	Reading & Language Arts	Reading & Language Arts	Reading & Language Arts	Reading & Language Arts	Reading & Language Arts
10:40-11:20 (30 min.)	History	Geography	History	Geography	History
11:20-12:10 (30 min.)	Science	Science	Science	Science	Science
12:10-12:40 (30 mins)	Lunch and Recess	Lunch and Recess	Lunch and Recess	Lunch and Recess	Lunch and Recess
12:40-1:00 (20 min.)	Literature	Literature	Literature	Literature	Literature
1:00-1:30 (30 min.)	Music	Physical Education	Dance	Physical Education	Art
1:30-2:00 (30 min.)	Enrichment Activities	Enrichment Activities	Enrichment Activities	Enrichment Activities	Enrichment Activities
2:00-2:30 (30 min.)	Worship, prayer, & praise	Worship, prayer, & praise	Worship, prayer, & praise	Worship, prayer, & praise	Worship, prayer, & praise

Step 7. Select your resources. It is important to make a list of your resources at the planning stage of the unit so you will have everything you need. Be very specific so you are well prepared in case something happens to disrupt your original plan. I like to have a closet with various science projects and tools available, but if you do not have storage, just bring in what you need the week you need it. When homeschooling, you have everything at your disposal or can take a field trip to the store as needed, but being prepared ahead of time is a great advantage and saves time in the long run.

Step 8. Plan student assessment. Throughout the unit, consider what evidence will show that you have met your intents. This is so very important! It is not enough to lecture and then have students regurgitate the key points you taught them. This kind of learning is easily taught and easily forgotten. The kind of enriched learning we are talking about in Kingdom education is lifelong learning. We want our students to love learning and find it exciting and fun. That is why we plan assessments throughout the lessons, not just as a culmination of the unit. Assessments can be informal. Students can dissect a flower and label the key structures like the stem, leaves, petals, etc. They can make a collection of leaves and identify different trees by the shape and design of the leaves. They can do an experiment they design themselves and practice the steps of the scientific method. The possibilities are endless. Use your imagination and follow the guidelines you set up in your unit planning. Be sure the assessments align with the unit focus. For instance, one of my unit outcomes was, "To help them fall deeper in love with God as the creator and sustainer of all things." This is a behavioral objective and is not easily measured with paper and pencil quizzes or tests. However, using a reason question and having the students write their reflections is a great way to assess this. For instance, "How have you seen the hand of God in our study of botany?" This gives them an open door to share their awe and love for God.

Step 9. Review the effectiveness of your unit. One of the most important things we forget in our teaching is to evaluate our effectiveness. To think governmentally, we use the simple phrase, "I plan, I do, I judge." We saw it in creation when God said, "Let there be light," "then there was light," and "God saw that it was good" (Gen 1). God plans, He does, and He judges. We are to follow His example. We spend a lot of time brainstorming and planning our lessons. It is equally important to make notes about what worked well and what didn't. Every time we develop a new unit, we need to judge how well it worked. You might want to take pictures of some of the best experiments and add them to your notebook. As you teach, the Holy Spirit will reveal new truths to you, and you should write them down to share the next time you teach it. The practice of evaluating our teaching helps to develop our skills and make us more prepared the next time we teach the unit. Here is an example of a completed self-evaluation for the botany lesson.

Self-Evaluation

THIS WENT WELL	NEXT TIME I WILL CHANGE THIS
Children really entered into the discussion from Genesis and shared some great insights into why we need seeds to reproduce after their own kinds.	
They loved the experiment with the seeds.	Have extra lima bean seeds available so they can take one home and show their families what they learned.
They enjoyed the poem and wanted to write more of their own, which led to a follow up lesson.	Have books of poetry as well as botany available. We didn't get time to sort the seeds, so we will save this for another day. Children were very curious about all the new pictures and books. Maybe save this for a later lesson next time.

Examples for Public School Teachers

Some of you reading may say this would be ideal teaching, but you teach in a public school setting and could never do what I am recommending. Many of you have strong government control even if you are a private school. First, let me applaud you for reading this book! You are the secret Kingdom God is using to touch the majority of children. Remember, you set the tone for your classroom. You can love your children and believe in them. You can pray daily and ask the Holy Spirit to empower you and to open up doors to share your faith. If you ask questions in such a way that the students ask you about your faith and you are free to share it. We also teach more about God by the way we respect and honor others than we do with our words about God. So, don't lose heart. God has you right where He wants you.

Here are some ideas of how you can introduce Kingdom principles without offending. Start by teaching your children to think cause to effect. In whatever subject you teach, focus on training your students to think. Any rational being will come to the conclusion eventually that there must be a God (Rom 1:20). In science, introduce the concept of intelligent design. Some wonderful resources are the Institute for Creation Research, Answers in Genesis, Moody Bible science clips, etc.

Another way is to introduce your students to men and women of character. In history, literature, reading, writing, etc. help them see that the decisions we make have consequences. For instance, you can use national holidays to promote men of character. In February in America, we celebrate President's Day. This is a great opportunity to talk about George Washington and what a godly leader he was. You might need to research the men and women who influenced your culture for good or for evil and talk to the students about how our choices lead to our life decisions. A great tool is the T-chart. On the left you write "Cause" and on the right you write "Effect." You can use this for history and other subjects as well. You start with the effect and then discuss what caused this to happen. For instance, George Washington was our first president. What caused him to be unanimously elected by all his peers? That leads to a discussion of his character. You ask leading questions to guide the discussion. You briefly record what the students contribute and, afterwards, ask them to copy it in their own handwriting and share what they learned with someone else. This helps them to continue to process the idea that character affects our choices. In the last chapter, there is an example of a T-chart on Noah Webster, but you can use it with any individual you study. Here is an example of a T-chart on George Washington that was prepared by a seven-year-old I tutored in Kingdom principles. His name is Isaiah Roseland and this is used with his permission. We start with the external first and then discuss how this came about, what character was needed to make this happen in his life.

George Washington

Internal	External
Perseverance as shown at Valley Forge when he could have gone into winter quarters but stayed with his men	"First in War" Leader of the colonial army
Servant leader-helped the men build their shelters Prayed in the snow Humble-refused to be king	"First in Peace" 1st President of the United States, unanimously elected by all
Honorable Honest Trustworthy Died because he put other's needs before his own Respectful of others People always coming to Mt. Vernon to visit him, even today	"First in the hearts of his countrymen"

You can also use the T-chart to study key events in history. You might want to research how and when missionaries came to your nation and how it affected your nation for good or for evil. These kinds of discussions are allowed even in public schools and you shouldn't be intimidated by your peers not to share them with your students. Remember Paul and Silas rejoiced that they were worthy to suffer persecution for their faith (Acts 5:41). If your act of boldness leads one child to faith it will be worth it all.

Another way you can bring Kingdom principles into your classroom is to share your love for each individual child in your care. One way to do this is through encouraging them to make individual timelines of their life. The children get pictures and talk to family and relatives about the people who influenced their lives. Then schedule different children to share their stories throughout the year. This is a wonderful way to get to know them better and let them know that you care about them. No one wants to know how much you know until they know how much you care. Help them to feel loved and cherished by you and by God. Teach your children to be good listeners when others are sharing. Help them appreciate *God's principle of individuality* even if you can't use that phrase freely. By demonstrating the value of each child, you are showing them unconditional love, which only comes through Christ. It opens up doors for you to share that you are a Christian when the time is right and the Holy Spirit prompts you to do so. I would also suggest you share your own timeline as an example. This gives you another way to share how important your faith is to you.

Examples for Christian School Teachers

THANK YOU FOR READING ON AND NOT THROWING IN THE TOWEL already. I have taught in Christian schools for more than thirty years and have experience with many different curricula. I know that, sometimes, you are the hardest audience of all to reach with Kingdom principles because you are already sacrificing so much to be teaching in a Christian school and you already have a good curriculum. What I am suggesting is to make good better and better best! If you are using a traditional Christian curriculum, you probably rely heavily on teacher lectures and students working independently in workbooks. I have already discussed why this methodology is not the best, but it is okay to use as a starting point if that is what you have been given. Students do see Bible verses on most textbook pages, but, unfortunately, they usually just skip over them. Most Christian curriculum is secular with Scriptures added. What I want to suggest to you is to begin with what you have and enrich the study to make it better. When your administration hired you, they gave you authority over your class, and the parents have given you their authority to train their children in the way they should go. The suggestions I will include here are in addition to everything I have mentioned already. The key is to start slowly and do that part well. With so many papers to grade, it is hard for you to find time to do a lot of independent unit writing, but the more you can, the better your results will be.

When I first began learning about Kingdom principles I was using a traditional Christian curriculum. The day was pretty well planned out for me, and I didn't see how I could fit anything else in. You might find yourself in a similar situation. I started by adding a literature book. When my students came back in after lunch, I would have them put their heads on their desks for a quiet time and I would read to them. We started with *The Lion, the Witch, and the Wardrobe* by CS Lewis. By introducing classical literature, you begin to develop in your students a love for the greatest and best of world culture. We didn't take notes, or fill in any worksheets, we just enjoyed the story together. At the end of the whole book we celebrated by watching the movie. We talked about how it was similar to the book and how it was different. It was a beginning and the students wanted more. They began to request longer times for reading, and I then said, "Well, if you want to hear more, then you will have to write and let the principal know why you think this kind of literature is so valuable to you." That led to a writing project and the students requested permission to read good books instead of the short compilation of stories they were used to. Try it and see what happens. As you get more comfortable with it, I would suggest you have a literature notebook. Ask the students to draw sketches of the scenes they see in their mind's eye as you read to them. Then ask them to write about their favorite characters and why they like them. Ask what they can learn from the choices they make. As you are able, you can introduce all the elements of good literature: setting, plot, characters, theme, and reason questions. Then enrich the study with a special day of celebration when the students can display their notebooks and sketches to their friends and family.

Next, I would suggest you take your favorite subject, one that you would enjoy studying and researching and begin there. It can be math, history, geography, etc. Whatever you enjoy most because your students will catch your enthusiasm. Start by adding some key individual studies to the curriculum. Create a timeline around the walls of your classroom and add the key individuals you study. Talk about how they fit into God's big plan for His kingdom work. Let your students know that each of them has a place in His-story too. Encourage the brighter students to do some key individual book reports and share what they learn with the rest of the class. In most traditional Christian school classrooms, gifted students are bored and spend a lot of free time either getting into trouble or just reading books they enjoys. Put these gifts to use by letting them be your research assistants. They get a chance to shine and actually do some of the work for you. You can ask to have copies made of their work and put it in your notebook for next time you teach it.

Examples for Homeschooling

The beauty of homeschooling is that you have the freedom to explore any subject that interests you and enrich it through wholistic teaching: creation, science, math, art, music, literature, field studies, etc. You can truly teach Kingdom curriculum with the Bible as the textbook that guides all your teaching. You don't have to create lesson plans and pass standardized tests. You don't need to waste time lining up and getting everyone's attention, so you can cover so much more ground. Whatever you love you can explore together as a family. You can go on lots of field study tours and see history come alive for your children. You can go to museums and library programs and meet with other homeschooling families to support each other. I know it is a lot of work, but it is an investment that pays eternal dividends.

Let's begin with the book of Proverbs. You can study one Proverb each day or take your time and really mine the depths of its wisdom by taking it slower. The beauty of homeschooling is you can truly be led by the Holy Spirit in this and all decisions as you don't need to answer to a board or administrator. I chose Proverbs because it is the book of wisdom. We will just use chapter one and show how you can begin to develop a rich study with God's Word as your foundation, not just an add-on to a secular curriculum.

I'm going to introduce you to a simple Bible study tool called the SOAP Method. It is an acronym for S-Scripture, O-Observations, A-Application, and P-Prayer. **Scripture** – Begin by praying and asking the Holy Spirit to guide you. Then read the whole chapter through in one sitting. Meditate on what you read. Go back and read it again slowly. This time, ask yourself, "what is God speaking to my heart about from this passage?" Begin to write down the verses that you felt were most significant. Each time you read it, you will get other things that stick out to you, as the Word is alive, active, and sharper than any two-edged sword (Hebrews 4:12). **Observation** – Look for key vocabulary that might need to be explained or defined for your children and write them down. What recurring phrases or themes do you observe? What do you see in the verses? What is God revealing to your heart through His Word? Take notes. This is similar to the researching phase of the notebook method. **Application** – How can you apply this truth to your life? This is where so many Christian school curricula fall short. They never bring the student to the "so what?" What does God actually want to teach me through this verse? How can I use it in my daily life to change me into the person God wants me to be? **Prayer** – We begin with prayer and we end our lesson with prayer. Write out a prayer asking God to help you implement what you have learned and make it alive for your children as you teach them what God is speaking into your heart. Allow room for the Holy Spirit to speak to your children also. There is no little Holy Spirit for children. God speaks just as clearly to them as He does to you and sometimes they are more able to hear His voice. Let them share with you their prayers too. Do this as a family.

I had a friend do this chapter also and this is what she gleaned as her life lessons: 1. The fear of the Lord (vs. 7), 2. Parental instruction (vs. 8-9), and 3. Disassociate with the wicked (vs. 10-19). The beauty is there are no right or wrong answers. Each person will hear what the Holy Spirit is teaching them. As you open up your teaching to His leading, He promises to show up. He is the master teacher. Here are a few insights I gleaned from this chapter. It is just an example, not an exhaustive study.

S.O.A.P. Bible Study Method

S - Scripture

Read Proverbs 1

"Which scripture stuck out the most?"

Proverbs 1:1-6 The purpose of the Proverbs

The proverbs of Solomon son of David, king of Israel:

[2] for gaining wisdom and instruction; for understanding words of insight; [3] for receiving instruction in prudent behavior, doing what is right and just and fair; [4] for giving prudence to those who are simple, [a] knowledge and discretion to the young— [5] let the wise listen and add to their learning, and let the discerning get guidance— [6] for understanding proverbs and parables, the sayings and riddles of the wise.

"The fear of the Lord is the beginning of knowledge, but fools[c] despise wisdom and instruction." Prov. 1:7

"My child, listen when your father corrects you. Don't neglect your mother's instruction. What you learn from them will crown you with grace and be a chain of honor around your neck." Proverbs 1:8,9 NLT

O - Observations

What recurring phrases or themes do you observe?

Define *Prudence* - Wisdom applied to practice. Prudence implies more caution and reserve than wisdom, or is exercised more in foreseeing and avoiding evil, than in devising and executing that which is good. It is sometimes mere caution or circumspection.

Repeating words or phrases:

Fear of the Lord

Wisdom

Instruction

Listen

Hate evil

Knowledge

What do you see in the verses?

The fear of the Lord is the beginning of knowledge, but fools despise wisdom and instruction.

Parental authority is emphasized in verses 8 & 9.

Listen, and lots of other action verbs.

Sinful men entice you but wisdom cries out openly.

Evil is the same in every generation.

Ill-gotten gain takes your life in the end and hurts you rather than helping you.

What is God revealing to your heart through His Word?

Seek wisdom first. It leads to prosperity and true happiness. God's ways are so much higher than our ways and His thoughts than our thoughts.

The wise become even wiser.

A - Application

How can you apply this truth to your life?

Key Thoughts:

Deceitfulness of the wicked is the same Greedy for money robs you of life Wisdom is calling but people ignore her When trouble comes we call for help then but it is too late We choose not to fear the LORD We reap what we sow Fools are destroyed by their own complacency

Not if disaster comes but when

Take away:

God offers us wisdom. It begins with the fear of the Lord. First, we must have a right relationship with God. We must love Him and fear Him. He is not your buddy or chum, He is the Sovereign creator God of the Universe and He chooses to spend time instructing us.

Wisdom is freely given, but it costs us everything. We must seek Him early and learn to fear the Lord as a young child. We are to follow the instructions of our parents as they teach us the fear of the Lord and show us how to go so we can avoid the pitfalls of sin.

P - Prayer

Lord, teach me to fear you and walk in your wisdom. Thank you that you give it so freely to all who seek you. Help me to train the next generation in the fear of the Lord. Help me to add to the wisdom you have already given me and to become wiser as I seek you daily through an intimate relationship and studying your precious Word..

. . .

THIS IS THE LAUNCHING PAD TO BEGIN DEVELOPING THE ENRICHED lessons we discussed earlier. Here are some suggestions, but feel free to run wild and enjoy whatever works for you and your family.

For **history**, I would start with an Old Testament review of who Solomon was and where he fit into the history of Israel. If your family has never gone to a "Walk Through the Bible" course together, I would highly recommend it. They talk about the kings of Israel in this way: "Saul – no heart; David – whole heart; and Solomon – half-heart." David was a man after God's own heart. He was a wonderful example of a man completely sold out to God. Read the Psalms to get a feel of how he worshipped God throughout his lifetime. Solomon started out right. He knew he needed wisdom to rule God's people well and that is what he asked for in I Kings 3:3-13. You can make a timeline of Old Testament history together (art and history). You can use a T-chart and look at some of the key events in Solomon's life and see what caused his actions. There are lots of ways to go with this. Again, just have fun!

For **literature**, you could begin a study of Proverbs and wise sayings. Almost every culture has this genre. America has Benjamin Franklin and Poor Richard's Almanac. Greece has Aesop's Fables. Egypt and Babylon also had written proverbs at the same time Solomon was writing. Your older children could do some research and share what they are learning with the other family members. For a younger child, I would recommend *Pinocchio* by Carlo Collodi. This book shows how Pinocchio was led astray by evil companions. You could study the **geography** of Italy and have a special day with foods, art, and music.

For **science**, you can study biology. Solomon collected thousands of proverbs and studied biology according to I Kings 4: 32-34. "He spoke three thousand proverbs and his songs numbered a thousand and five. He spoke about plant life, from the cedar of Lebanon to the hyssop that grows out of walls. He also spoke about animals: birds, reptiles, and fish. From all nations people came to listen to Solomon's wisdom, sent by all the kings of the world, who had heard of his wisdom."

Study the things that your children enjoy. Go on field trips to the zoo, botanical gardens, take walks in the woods, and explore the world around you. Have your children keep field journals and write what they observe. Have them sketch and draw what they see.

In the next chapter, we will go into what this looks like if you are able to start from scratch and do full blown Kingdom education. You can use all the ideas we have already shared or you can begin with the Word of God and synthesize Kingdom principles and develop your curriculum around them.

KINGDOM CURRICULUM APPLIED

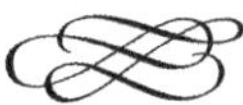

The first words of Jesus after his baptism and temptation when he began his ministry were, "Repent of your sins and turn to God, for the Kingdom of Heaven is near" (Matt 4:17). That is where we also should begin our teaching. We need to call our students to repentance from sin and a turning to God. The Kingdom of God is entered into as a little child. Matthew 18:3 says, "Verily I say unto you, except you be converted, and become as little children, you shall not enter into the Kingdom of heaven." It is based on a relationship with God through Jesus.

In order for our children to come to God, they first must know who God is. I recommend starting with the sovereignty of God. We begin in the beginning with Genesis. This lays a foundation for everything else we study. Genesis begins with the assumption that God is preexistent. It doesn't explain where God came from because He has always existed. In the book of Genesis, we see the unity and plurality of the trinity. God says, "Let us make man in our image." We see the Holy Spirit hovering over the waters. In the book of John, chapter one, we see that Jesus was in the beginning and all things were made by Him.

In Kingdom education, we do not shirk from introducing our students to these very deep theological teachings.

The key to Kingdom education is relationship. We want our students to fall in love with God and honor Him in everything they do. Therefore, we place a strong emphasis on the two great commandments. Jesus said the whole law and the prophets, meaning the whole Old Testament, can be summed up in these two commands, to love God and to love your neighbor as yourself (Matt 22:36-40). If we are to really love our neighbors as ourselves, it is implied that we also will have a healthy self-love. Therefore, we will develop a loving nurturing environment where students can grow in their relationship with God and each other. We will practice the art of forgiveness. We will teach servant leadership. We will focus on developing Christian character. All these kingdom concepts will be taught though the avenue of academics.

If both secular and Kingdom education teach academics, then how are we uniquely different? In Kingdom education, we use the academics as the platform to bring the Kingdom principles to life. Academics are secondary to the Word of God and the Kingdom principles. We are training our students to rule and reign with Christ and to understand the rules that govern God's kingdom, which are often contrary to the way the world works in the natural. We start with the end in mind and build the curriculum experiences around the principles we are trying to teach. In the next chapter, we will go step by step through how you can do this.

The main goal of Jewish education was holiness in response to a living relationship with God. "Ye shall be holy, for I the Lord your God am holy" and "Sanctify yourselves therefore and be ye holy; for I am the Lord your God" (Lev 19:2; 20:7, 26). The Jewish ideal of education is holiness, separation from other peoples in order to belong to God. "Their educational system was nothing less than the instrument by which their existence as a nation, and their fulfillment of their destiny, was ensured" (Barclay, 1974, p. 47). The Jewish educational ideal was to fit the child to be a servant of God. This model of education holds great promise for transforming lives today and will be an integral part of Kingdom education.

The early church adopted the Hebrew model of education (Barclay, 1974). It participated in community building through taking responsibility for one another's needs, as demonstrated in Acts 2:42-47. The New Testament uses the Greek word *koinonia* (Strong's #2842), which means 'partnership, that is, (literally) participation, or (social) intercourse, or (pecuniary) benefaction—(to) communicate, communion, distribution, fellowship.' The church accepted responsibility to train the children in order to pass on the faith. Seymour and Miller (1990) explained this community of believers in this way:

> It means to be with another, to claim another's joys and sorrows as our own (Rom 12:15). It means we lay ourselves open to what others are going through, and go through it with them (Hebrews 13:3). It means to care, to be there, to be vulnerable, to be compassionate. (p. 142)

This sense of the whole community being responsible for one another is not as prevalent in the modern church, but this is one of the goals of Kingdom education — to restore this wholistic, communal responsibility for learning by training multiple generations including parents, teachers, and significant others in the community. Doug Phillips (as cited in Schutte, 2004), founder of The Vision Forum, Inc., proclaimed:

> We must have a system of education which is intensely personal, familistic and relationship driven "so that virtue is added to faith, and knowledge to virtue, as required by Scripture" (2 Pet 1:5); a system that trains the believer to "think God's thoughts after Him" through a presuppositionally biblical approach to truth; a system which rejects the idea that either our methods or our philosophy of education are neutral; and a system which emphasizes that the supreme goal of

> education is not simply to fill the mind with facts, or to get a credential, but to see the child "transformed after the image of the God who made him. (¶ 4)

We are proposing this kind of relational education. The Bible lays the responsibility for training primarily on the parents. Parents are responsible for the training of their children in the ways of the Lord (Deut 6; Proverbs 22:6). The church is responsible for equipping parents to do this job well (Eph 4). The school is a delegated authority, which receives permission from parents for training *in loco parentis* (in place of the parents). The ideal is when the home, school, and church work together in community to train the next generation. This is Kingdom education at its best.

In the next chapter, we will lay the foundation for building caring Kingdom communities using relationship building principles (RBP) I developed during my doctoral dissertation. I researched best practices from school effectiveness research (SER), teacher effectiveness research (TER), Brain research, multiple intelligence findings, as well as other nonbiblical research (Hameloth, 2011). I synthesized these into 18 relationship building principles. I recommend these as a starting point to create communities of care within the Kingdom school movement.

RELATIONSHIP-BUILDING PRINCIPLES

Before you begin this chapter, it is important that you realize that this is the ideal. You may not be able to achieve it at first, but it is something to strive for. Create checkpoints and ask the Holy Spirit to show you what you need to focus on as a school community. If you are just beginning you have a blank slate and can choose which of these relationship building principles are most important in your situation. The way the chapter is laid out is that I state the relationship building principle, then I define the key terms. Next, I give the Biblical support for the principle. I follow up with the literature support. Finally, I give a few examples of how to apply the principle to teaching in general. Most of these relationship-building principles can be applied whether you find yourself in a public, private, or home school setting.

1— "Love the LORD your God with all your heart and with all your soul and with all your strength" (Deut 6:5).

Define Key Terms Within the RBP

Barclay (2001) explained love as the essence of the Christian ethic. He said there are four Greek words used for love in the New Testament: (a) eros, which is the love of passion; (b) sorge, which is the word for family love—the love of parents for child and child for parents; (c) phileo (Strong's #G5368), which is warm, affectionate love, including both spiritual and physical fellowship and intimacy; and (d) agape (Strong's #G26), which is God's love or unconquerable benevolence.

> *Agape* is not only a thing of the heart; it is also a thing of the will. It is not a mere happening; it is a conquest. It is something into which we must will ourselves, and can only will ourselves through the Spirit of Jesus Christ.... The demand of Christianity is a universal and unconquerable benevolence to all people, no matter what their attitude to us, and their treatment of us is (Matt 5:45). (Barclay, 2001, p. 5)

In order to love God well, one must understand who God is. He is the sovereign ruler over all the universe. Webster (1828) defined *sovereign* as "supreme in power; possessing supreme dominion; as a sovereign ruler of the universe...superior to all others; chief." God is the sovereign ruler of the universe and, therefore, it is important for teachers, parents, and children to focus on the nature of God as they begin to live in loving relationship with Him. Hayford (1995) recommended beginning a study of the kingdom of God by addressing God's sovereignty:

> God's Sovereignty (Gen 1:1). The necessary beginning point in studying the theme of "the kingdom of God" is the Bible's opening verse. Here we meet the Sovereign of all the universe, whose *realm, reign,* and *regency* are described at the outset. (1) His *realm* (or scope of His rule) is transcendent: that is, not only does it include the entire physical universe, it exceeds it. He existed before all creation. He expands beyond it, and by virtue of having begotten it, He encompasses all that it is. (2) His *reign* (or power by which He rules) is exercised by His will, His word, and His works. By His own will He creatively decides and designs; by His own word He speaks

> creation into being; and by His own works, His Spirit displays His unlimited power. (3) His *regency* (or authority to rule) is in His preexistence and holiness. He is there before creation "in the beginning." Thus, as its Creator, He deserves to be its Potentate. His benevolent intent in creating things "good" reveals His holy nature (that is, complete and perfect), and thus His moral right to be creation's King. All kingdom power and authority flow from Him. (p. 680)

God's sovereignty is foundational for building a loving relationship with Him. Man does not determine what God is like, God reveals Himself through creation (Rom 1:20), His Word (John 1:1), and His son (John 14:9). God is sovereign of the universe, and His realm, reign, and regency will be further explored as they are applied to Kingdom education.

Biblical Support for the RBP

Exodus 34:6: "And he passed in front of Moses, proclaiming, 'The LORD, the LORD, the compassionate and gracious God, slow to anger, abounding in love and faithfulness.'"

Deuteronomy 7:9, 12:

> Know therefore that the LORD your God is God; he is the faithful God, keeping his covenant of love to a thousand generations of those who love him and keep his commands.... If you pay attention to these laws and are careful to follow them, then the LORD your God will keep his covenant of love with you, as he swore to your forefathers.

John 16:27: "The Father himself loves you because you have loved me and have believed that I came from God."

Romans 1:7: "To all in Rome who are loved by God and called to be saints: Grace and peace to you from God our Father and from the Lord Jesus Christ."

Ephesians 5:1: "Be imitators of God, therefore, as dearly loved children."

Literature Support for the RBP

Erikson's (1950) initial stage of "trust verses mistrust." He believed the "infant" or foundational stage of development required that children needed "maximum comfort with minimal uncertainty to trust himself/herself, others, and the environment" (p.7). Although Erikson defined this stage as the "infant" stage, it is not just a chronological infant; all people must go through this succession of stages for mature adult personality development. Loving God and building a trusting relationship with Him is foundational for all other relationships. When one trusts the sovereign God to guide and direct one's steps, then it is easier to learn to trust others.

Chapman (2002) shared that God is a relational God, and He desires to spend quality time with His children. If a person loves God, he will seek to live in a loving relationship with Him and His creation. Submission to authority is a natural outcome of loving God and understanding His sovereignty. "The reality is there can be no peace... if we are not living in keeping with the Creator's design. It is... choosing to obey the rules of God because we believe that they are designed for our well-being" (Chapman, 2002, p. 172).

Elliot (1999) said children must have the understanding and knowledge of spiritual dimensions: "Children's readiness to believe, their inclination to worship, and their acceptance of authority predispose them to respond to God" (Wilkerson, as cited in Elliot, 1999, p. 87). The sovereignty of God helps parents and teachers establish the reason for all authority. Mankind is made in the image of God and is commissioned to be vice-regents of His creation.

Examples of How to Apply the RBP to Teaching in General

Teachers can love God through worship. Their example will be a role model for the children and parents to emulate.

Teachers can love God by serving Him well. Diligence to the profession of teaching is an act of loving worship to the creator of all things.

Teachers can love God through praying in the Spirit and with their understanding (Eph 6:18) throughout the day for wisdom to know how to teach well.

Teachers can love God by loving others. As they work to develop loving relationships with others in the family of God, they are ministering to God Himself (Mark 9:37).

2— Love others unconditionally (1 Cor 13).

Define Key Terms Within the RBP

Love is defined from a biblical perspective in the previous RBP. Webster (1828) further defined love:

> In a general sense to be pleased with; to regard with affection, on account of some qualities which excite pleasing sensations or desire of gratification... In short, we love whatever gives us pleasure and delight, whether animal or intellectual; and if our hearts are right, we love God above all things, as the sum of all excellence and all the attributes which can communicate happiness to intelligent beings. In other words, the Christian loves God with the love of complacency in his attributes, the love of benevolence towards the interest of his kingdom, and the love of gratitude for favors received.

A recent study by Dartmouth Medical School and the YMCA USA found, "We are biologically primed to connect with other people and with moral and spiritual meaning and that individuals who follow these biological cues are likely to be significantly healthier and happier than individuals who do not" (Bavolek, 2003, p. 4). The goal of Kingdom curriculum is to help children, parents, and teachers connect with one another in meaningful ways and grow in a loving relationship with God and others.

Biblical Support for the RBP

First Corinthians 13: 4-8:

Love is patient, love is kind. It does not envy, it does not boast, it is not proud. It is not rude, it is not self-seeking, it is not easily angered, it keeps no record of wrongs. Love does not delight in evil but rejoices with the truth. It always protects, always trusts, always hopes, always perseveres. Love never fails.

Leviticus 18:19: "Do not seek revenge or bear a grudge against one of your people, but love your neighbor as yourself. I am the LORD."

Galatians 5:14: "The entire law is summed up in a single command: Love your neighbor as yourself."

James 2:8: "If you really keep the royal law found in Scripture, 'Love your neighbor as yourself,' you are doing right."

Literature Support for the RBP

Stronge, Tucker, and Hindman (2003) emphasized the need for creating a safe and caring environment in order for students to feel safe to take academic risks:

Research reveals that effective teachers differentiate instruction; develop clear goals for student learning and link classroom activities to them; make the most of instructional time through smooth transitions and limited disruptions; and create situations in which students can succeed and feel safe in taking academic risks. (p. 53)

This is supported through RBP #11, recognize the distinctive talents. It also aligns with RBP #4, nurture the imago Dei qualities, and RBP #2, love others unconditionally.

Friesen et al. (2000) established the need for unconditional love for children to thrive. Since education deals with real children who are developmentally different, the more focus on sound developmental praxis, the more safe and secure the children will feel. Children's most basic need is to feel unconditional love. They need to know that someone is delighted just because they exist.

Examples of How to Apply the RBP to Teaching in General

Teachers can love children unconditionally by showing delight when they arrive at school, always putting aside whatever other things they are focusing on, and greeting each child by name and welcoming them into the classroom with joy.

Teachers can love parents unconditionally by listening to their suggestions and helping them to feel a part of the training team. Honoring parents and helping them feel welcomed in the classroom also conveys unconditional love.

Teachers can love fellow teachers unconditionally by expecting the best every day and not keeping a record of wrongs. We need to treat others the way we want to be treated with honor, respect, unconditional acceptance, and pure love (1 Cor 13).

3— Depend on the Holy Spirit for guidance.

Define Key Terms Within the RBP

The Holy Spirit is the third person in the Trinity (John 14:16, 26). Hayford (1995) said we know God through the ministry of the Holy Spirit "who makes a personal relationship with Christ, and a growing knowledge of Him possible by faith (John 15:26-27; 16:7-15; I Corinthians 12:3; Romans 8:11)" (p. 622). Through the Holy Spirit, the body of Christ receives various gifts to ensure its unity (1 Cor 12:4-27). He makes intercessions for us with groanings that cannot be spoken (Rom 8:26, 27). He reveals the deep things of God (1 Cor 2:10-12). This is just a beginning study of the ministry of the Holy Spirit.

Biblical Support for the RBP

John 16:13: "But when He, the Spirit of truth, comes, He will guide you into all truth. He will not speak on His own; He will speak only what He hears, and He will tell you what is yet to come."

John 14:26: "But the Counselor, the Holy Spirit, whom the Father will send in my name, will teach you all things and will remind you of everything I have said to you."

Literature Support for the RBP

Palmer (1997) referred to good teaching as that which comes from the integrity of the teacher. Teaching is an art that deals with the intellect, emotion, and spiritual dimensions. "Intellectual pedagogy deals with the way one teaches; emotion deals with feelings that can either enlarge or diminish others; and spiritual means answering the heart's longing to be connected with the largeness of life" (Palmer, 1997, p. 2). The Holy Spirit will guide the teacher to know how to be sensitive to the climate in the classroom (Rom 8).

Based on the findings of TER, "An effective teacher employs pedagogical procedural information useful in enhancing learner-focused teaching" (Grimmett & MacKinnon, 1992, p. 387). Teachers are expected to draw on both pedagogical content knowledge, as well as knowledge of each student, to optimize student learning (Harris & Rutledge, 2007). This model requires an emphasis on the student–teacher relationship. The Holy Spirit, as the master teacher, will guide the classroom teacher and parents to know what is best for each child.

Examples of How to Apply the RBP to Teaching in General

Teachers can love others unconditionally by accepting each person for who they are as children of God and not judging them harshly.

Teachers can love fellow teachers by spending time with them during lunch or breaks and looking for ways to serve them.

Teachers can love the parents by doing a good job of loving their children. As we practice loving others, it becomes a reflection of how much God loves us, and those who are not yet believers may be drawn to serve our loving God.

. . .

4— Nurture the imago Dei qualities.

Define Key Terms Within the RBP

We are made in the image of God (Gen 1:26) and have all the rights and responsibilities of fulfilling our destiny (Psalm 8:6). This leads to an understanding of the relational nature of God through studying the Trinity and building a loving relationship with God and others, who are also made in His image.

The imago Dei is a complicated subject that will require a lifelong study. However, it can be broken down into some basic understandings that even a young child can grasp. Hayford (1995) reflected on human worth and divine destiny by saying, "Though incapable of saving himself, man—as creature—represents God's highest and best, made in His image and intended for His glory" (p. 659). The significant value God places on humankind is evident in His willingness to sacrifice His only son for mankind's salvation (I Peter 1:18-19). Man is a spiritual and moral being. His "intelligence, perception, and self-determination far exceed that of any other earthly being" (Hayford, p. 659). God designed humans to have unique personalities. He gave them "both freedom and the awareness to respond to God, to other human beings, and to the environment" (Hayford, p. 660).

Webster (1828) defined *image* as "a representation or similitude of any person or thing, formed of a material substance." God made man to be His image bearers. The *Reformation Study Bible* states what it means to be made in the image of God this way: "Humans in their whole beings —body and soul—truly represent God (Psalm 94:10), possess His life and so have the potential for intimacy with Him" (pp. 8-9). The image of God is associated with royalty. Mankind is chosen to bear God's image on earth and act as His representatives having dominion over all creation.

Biblical Support for the RBP

Genesis 1:26-28:

> Then God said, "Let us make man in our image, in our likeness, and let them rule over the fish of the sea and the birds of the air, over the livestock, over all the earth, and over all the creatures that move along the ground." So God created man in his own image, in the image of God he created him; male and female he created them. God blessed them and said to them, "Be fruitful and increase in number; fill the earth and subdue it. Rule over the fish of the sea and the birds of the air and over every living creature that moves on the ground."

Hebrews 2:6-8: "What is man that you are mindful of him, the son of man that you care for him? You made him a little lower than the angels; you crowned him with glory and honor and put everything under his feet."

Literature Support for the RBP

Several researchers both in the SER and TER emphasize the need for high expectations. As teachers are accountable for student performance, they take responsibility for setting and maintaining high expectations for student success. Having staff members hold high expectations for themselves as leaders and teachers, taking responsibility for student performance (Brookover & Lezotte, 1982; Edmonds, 1979; Murphy & Hallinger, 1985). This is supported by RBP #4, nurture the imago Dei qualities.

Murphy and Hallinger (1985) stated, "Perhaps the most important thing schools can do to promote high expectations is to frame school purpose policies in terms of one or two academic goals, which can, in turn, provide the framework for all other school activity" (p. 24). As students realize they are made in the image of God (RBP #4), they will take ownership for setting and accomplishing high academic goals. They are charged by God to have dominion over His creation (Gen 1:28); therefore, they will need to focus their attention on accomplishing academic success to glorify God (1 Cor 10:31).

According to *Matthew Henry's Commentary* (1706), God's image upon man consists of these three things:

> (a) In his nature and constitution, not those of his body (for God has not a body), but those of his soul...(b) in his place and authority: *Let us make man in our image, and let him have dominion.* As he has the government of the inferior creatures, he is, as it were, God's representative, or viceroy, upon earth...and (c) In his purity and rectitude. God's image upon man consists in knowledge, righteousness, and true holiness (Eph 4:24; Colossians 3:10). (pp. 11-12)

Cox et al. (1999) further defined the imago Dei as elements of God's nature. Some of these God-image qualities that humans possess include socialization, dignity, trust, security, righteousness, authority, self-discipline, worship, dominion, perfection, creativity, competence, destiny, purpose, and love.

Examples of How to Apply the RBP to Teaching in General

Teachers can nurture the imago Dei qualities by treating each child as a person of utmost worth. Listening carefully when they talk to you, looking directly at them, smiling, and showing approval and love all help nurture the imago Dei.

Teachers nurture the imago Dei qualities by holding high expectations for students. Realizing they are made in the image of God allows teachers to treat students as creative, inventive, capable students.

Teachers can nurture the imago Dei qualities by asking for and using feedback given from children, parents, and other members of the teaching community.

5— Discipline in love based on the principles of God's Word.

Define Key Terms Within the RBP

Webster (1828) defined *discipline* as "to instruct or educate; to inform the mind; to prepare by instructing in correct principles and habits; as, to discipline youth for a profession, or for future usefulness... to correct; to chastise; to punish." One of the Hebrew words for discipline is *yâsar* (Strong's #H3256), which means "to chastise, literally (with blows) or figuratively (with words); hence to instruct: bind, chasten, chastise, correct, instruct, punish, reform, reprove, sore, teach." Therefore, biblical discipline involves correction as well as instruction.

Biblical Support for the RBP

Deuteronomy 8:5: "Know then in your heart that as a man disciplines his son, so the LORD your God disciplines you."

Psalm 94:12: "Blessed is the man you discipline, O LORD, the man you teach from your law."

Proverbs 6:23: "For these commands are a lamp, this teaching is a light, and the corrections of discipline are the way to life."

Proverbs 13:24: "He who spares the rod hates his son, but he who loves him is careful to discipline him."

Ephesians 6:4: "Fathers, do not exasperate your children; instead, bring them up in the training and instruction of the Lord."

Colossians 3:21: "Fathers, do not embitter your children, or they will become discouraged."

Literature Support for the RBP

Research supports children's most basic need is to feel unconditional love (Friesen et al., 2000). When children act out, due to the sin nature, it is important that teachers and parents love them unconditionally and separate the sinner from the sin. Biblical discipline and an emphasis on forgiveness are both necessary for unconditional love to thrive.

Discipline is a necessary part of education because of the sin nature.

Discipline or correction enhances self-control, which leads to subjugation of the sin nature. Change occurs when discomfort of correction exceeds pleasure of inappropriate behavior. The imago Dei flows toward surrender of self to God, while the sin nature flows toward edification of self (Cox, 2004).

The Hebrew word for instruction is *muwcar* (Strong's #H4148) and occurs about 30 times in Proverbs. It means both discipline and instruction. According to Strong (1890; 998, 2449, 2451, 2452, 2454, 2942, 3820, 4486, 4726, 5094, 6195, 7919, 7922, 8394, and 8454), wisdom teaches prudent forethought, temperance, chastity, diligence, truthfulness, consideration of the poor, a most unusual and truly noble charity to enemies, the value of true friendship, and the dignity of good womanhood (Proverbs 6:6-11; 7:6; 14:21; 17:7, 17; 18:24; 19:17; 21:17; 22:9; 23:20, 21, 29-35; 24:27; 25:21, 22; 27:10; 29:3; 31:10-31).

Examples of How to Apply the RBP to Teaching in General

Teachers can practice biblical discipline by setting firm guidelines that are clearly instructed throughout the year. High expectations for Christian self-government lead to students who take responsibility for their own actions and the natural consequences of those actions. Rules should be few and clearly communicated. When a child breaks a rule, there should be fair consequences that have been clearly articulated before the offense.

Teachers should work closely with parents to be sure the discipline in the classroom is formative and instructive. The goal of all biblical discipline is for children to govern themselves under God's authority. The teacher's job is to train the children in how to love God by obeying His commandments. This includes obeying teachers since they are a delegated authority appointed by God.

6— Use the five love languages (words of affirmation, gifts, quality time, acts of service, and physical touch; Chapman, 1997).

Define Key Terms Within the RBP

Gary Chapman (1997, 2002, 2005) produced an amazing series of books on the primary love languages. His premise is that there are five love languages, and each person has one that is primary. By speaking each child's primary love language, the teacher or parent can fill their emotional tank with unconditional love. Young children need all five to function fully, but as they grow and mature, one becomes their primary love language. God expresses His love to all in each person's primary love language. Following is just one example of each:

1. To those who understand the love language of words of affirmation, Jesus says, "Come to me, all you who are weary and burdened, and I will give you rest" (Matt 11:28).
2. To those whose primary love language is gifts, Jesus gives the gift of eternal life (John 3:16).
3. To those who desire quality time, the Scriptures say, "Come near to God and he will come to you" (James 4:8).
4. To those whose love language is acts of service, Jesus says of Himself, "The Son of Man did not come to be served, but to serve, and to give his life as a ransom for many" (Matt 20:28).
5. For those who understand best the love language physical touch, nothing speaks more profoundly than the incarnation of Christ. John the apostle described it as follows: "(What) we have heard...seen with our eyes...looked at and our hands have touched—this we proclaim" (Chapman, 2002, p. 214). Since learning is a relational activity, it succeeds best when a child is emotionally secure. This is accomplished through filling each child's emotional love tank (Chapman, 1997).

Biblical Support for the RBP

First John 3:18: "Dear children, let us not love with words or tongue but with actions and in truth."

First John 4:7-8: "Dear friends, let us love one another, for love comes from God. Everyone who loves has been born of God and knows God. Whoever does not love does not know God, because God is love."

Literature Support for the RBP

Chapman (1997) developed the five love languages. After many years of counseling couples, he discovered five key categories or five love languages. He believed everyone has a love language, and we all identify primarily with one of the five love languages: words of affirmation, quality time, receiving gifts, acts of service, and physical touch.

Examples of How to Apply the RBP to Teaching in General

Words of affirmation. Teachers have many opportunities throughout the day to express their love and concern to their students through words of affirmation: greetings, using each child's name, speaking directly to the child, praising for specific things and not just in generalities, and actually saying, "I love you."

Quality time. Teachers can spend quality time with the children by opting to sit with them at lunch or talk to them on the playground or other times when they are available such as before and after school.

Receiving gifts. Teachers can give inexpensive gifts like having a prize box where children can choose a small gift when they have done something appropriate to earn it. Giving stickers and having pencils or notebook paper available for their use also expresses love.

Acts of service. Teachers serve children all the time by grading their papers, reading the notes they send, and helping open milk at lunch, etc. Many children have trouble keeping their desks cleaned out, and one way to show love through acts of service would be to actually clean out their desks as a surprise and leave a little note saying, "I love you."

Physical touch. Teachers can hug younger children; but as children get older, it is more difficult. Still, a teacher can give a comforting pat on the back, ruffle the hair, etc.

. . .

7— Provide emotional security.

Define Key Terms Within the RBP

Dictionary.com defined *emotions* as "an affective state of consciousness in which joy, sorrow, fear, hate, or the like, is experienced, as distinguished from cognitive and volitional states of consciousness" (Emotions, 2010). Security means "freedom from care, anxiety, or doubt; well-founded confidence."

Biblical Support for the RBP

Ezekiel 34:1-3, 11-12:

> The word of the LORD came to me: Son of man, prophesy against the shepherds of Israel; prophesy and say to them: This is what the Sovereign LORD says: Woe to the shepherds of Israel who only take care of themselves! Should not shepherds take care of the flock? You eat the curds, clothe yourselves with the wool and slaughter the choice animals, but you do not take care of the flock...For this is what the Sovereign LORD says: I myself will search for my sheep and look after them. As a shepherd looks after his scattered flock when he is with them, so will I look after my sheep. I will rescue them.

Psalm 27:1, 13-14:

> The LORD is my light and my salvation—whom shall I fear? The LORD is the stronghold of my life—of whom shall I be afraid?...I am still confident of this: I will see the goodness of the LORD in the land of the living. Wait for the LORD; be strong and take heart and wait for the LORD.

Literature Support for the RBP

Brooks as cited in Cohen, 1999) contributed that "a sense of security and self-worth in a classroom provides the scaffolding that supports increased learning, motivation, self-discipline, realistic risk-taking, and the ability to deal effectively with mistakes" (p. 62).

Marlow (1977) suggested three ways this emotionally healthy environment can be created: (a) unconditional love with plenty of positive reinforcement, (b) realistic discipline that holds children responsible for their actions within the limits of their abilities, and (c) a support system that is dependable and truthful.

Brain research supports this principle: "Make the class emotionally, socially, and physically safe for learning" (Tirozzi, 2002, p. 78).

Examples of How to Apply the RBP to Teaching in General

Teachers can provide emotional support by loving each child unconditionally and helping them know that God loves them even more.

Teachers help provide emotional security by inviting parents to be a part of class often and making them feel welcome, not just on special occasions, but any time they want to just drop by. This helps parents feel more emotionally secure too.

8— Create a community of care through nurturing the whole person—spirit, soul, and body.

Define Key Terms Within the RBP

Webster (1828) defined *care* as "concern...solicitude...a looking to; regard; attention, or heed, with a view to safety or protection...implying concern for safety and prosperity." Communities imply connectivity. So communities of care are networks of people who look out for the welfare of others. It implies caring for the whole person: body, soul, and spirit. The foundation for creating communities of care is the unity found in the body of Christ. Webster defined *unity* as

> The state of being one; oneness and in Christian theology, oneness of

> sentiment, affection, or behavior: Unity of spirit, is the oneness which subsists between Christ and his saint, by which the same spirit dwells in both, and both have the same disposition and aims; and it is the oneness of Christians among themselves, united under the same head, having the same spirit dwelling in them, and possessing the same graces, faith, love, hope, etc.

Biblical Support for the RBP

First Peter 5:2-3:

> Be shepherds of God's flock that is under your care, serving as overseers—not because you must, but because you are willing, as God wants you to be; not greedy for money, but eager to serve; not lording it over those entrusted to you, but being examples to the flock.

Romans 12:9-10: "Love must be sincere. Hate what is evil; cling to what is good. Be devoted to one another in brotherly love. Honor one another above yourselves."

Ephesians 4:15-16:

> Instead, speaking the truth in love, we will in all things grow up into him who is the Head, that is, Christ. From him the whole body, joined and held together by every supporting ligament, grows and builds itself up in love, as each part does its work.

First Thessalonians 5:23: "May God himself, the God of peace, sanctify you through and through. May your whole spirit, soul and body be kept blameless at the coming of our Lord Jesus Christ."

Literature Support for the RBP

Harris and Rutledge (2007) discussed how the school leader functions in creating a community of care that nurtures the whole person.

> [He is] a person whose work as an educational leader is first, foremost

> and always with persons...who are physical, intellectual, spiritual, emotional and social beings...(and) building a community of learners in which all persons can flourish. (p. 166)

Friesen et al. (2000) researched the need for unconditional love in order for human beings to function fully. It takes an emotionally secure person to be able to love others well. Children need to know that someone is delighted just that they exist. Parents and family members first communicate this to the developing infant, but if it is neglected, there remains a gap in the emotional development of the child. Parents and teachers have an obligation to create safe, caring, and nurturing environments that help meet these basic needs.

Hayford (1995) discussed God's design for mankind as follows: "His majestic plan was to create distinctiveness within oneness...distinctive marks of the divine set him apart from other living beings (Gen 2:7)" (p. 708). Man is responsible under God to provide for the material, emotional, and spiritual needs of his mate. "Material provision, which includes food, clothing, and shelter; emotional provision, which involves love, security, and understanding; and spiritual provision, which stresses guidance, maturity, and sensitivity (Eph 5:23. 25-27; I Timothy 5:8)" (Hayford, p. 708).

Gardner (1999) discussed the need for a caring, nurturing environment: "It matters when teachers know their students well, can ask about their interests and families, comfort them in times of trouble...it matters when the members of a community...are courteous and helpful to one another" (p. 233).

Examples of How to Apply the RBP to Teaching in General

Teachers can create communities of care by being there for their students. When the children come into school in the morning, it is important to let each child know that you are thrilled that they have come and you expect to enjoy the day with them personally.

Teachers can create communities of care by nurturing the individuality of each student. Help each child know they have a unique destiny that only they can fulfill. Speak positively into their lives.

Help create communities of care by protecting each child from bullying both verbally and physically.

9— Reconcile persons to God and to one another in a supportive community.

Define Key Terms Within the RBP

Reconciling persons to God means bringing them into relationship with God through the redemption provided by Jesus Christ. Strong (1890) defined *redemption* (G629) as "ransom in full...Christian salvation, deliverance." Webster (1828) defined it as "in theology, the purchase of God's favor by the death and sufferings of Christ; the ransom or deliverance of sinners from the bondage of sin and the penalties of God's violated law by the atonement of Christ." Some clear Scriptures on redemption are Romans 3:24; Ephesians 1:7, 14; 4:30; Collosians 1:14; and Hebrews 9:12.

Biblical Support for the RBP

Romans 3:23-24:

> God presented him as a sacrifice of atonement, through faith in his blood. He did this to demonstrate his justice, because in his forbearance he had left the sins committed beforehand unpunished—he did it to demonstrate his justice at the present time, so as to be just and the one who justifies those who have faith in Jesus.

Ephesians 1:7, 14:

> In him we have redemption through his blood, the forgiveness of sins, in accordance with the riches of God's grace...who is a deposit

> guaranteeing our inheritance until the redemption of those who are God's possession—to the praise of his glory.

Ephesians 4:30: "And do not grieve the Holy Spirit of God, with whom you were sealed for the day of redemption."

Collosians 1:13-14: "For he has rescued us from the dominion of darkness and brought us into the kingdom of the Son he loves, in whom we have redemption, the forgiveness of sins."

Hebrews 9:12: "He did not enter by means of the blood of goats and calves; but he entered the Most Holy Place once for all by his own blood, having obtained eternal redemption."

Literature Support for the RBP

RBP #9, reconcile persons to God and to one another, is supported by authors like Barna (2006), Beechick (2004), Friesen et al. (2000), and Palmer (1998). One significant finding from the Barna's research on how 20-somethings walked away from their faith even though they were very active during their teenage years is to increase the application of a biblical worldview, which is one of the goals of Kingdom curriculum. Barna concluded,

> Another shift is to develop teenagers' ability to think and process the complexities of life from a biblical viewpoint. This is not so much about having the right head knowledge as it is about helping teens respond to situations and decisions in light of God's principles for life. Also, we have learned that effective youth ministries do not operate in isolation but have a significant role in training parents to minister to their own children. (¶ 17)

Examples of How to Apply the RBP to Teaching in General

Teachers can reconcile their students to God and build supportive communities by sharing the good news of the gospel whenever appropriate.

Teachers should also try to reconcile parents and others from the community to God by presenting the gospel message whenever there is an opportunity, like through Christmas pageants, spring concerts, end-of-year celebrations, etc.

10— Forgive others and yourself (Cox & Hameloth, 2003-2009; Ornish, 1998, 2005).

Define Key Terms Within the RBP

Forgiveness is needed in all human relationships.

> Forgiveness is the purposeful choice and commandment to not hold unto an offense whether or not given consciously and purposefully. There is no end to the number of times Jesus expects people to forgive others (Matt 18:22). While forgiveness may not always be vocally expressed to the offense giver, it must be expressed openly and sincerely to God, without reservation. Forgiveness to others is apparently a determinant of God's forgiveness to us (Matt 6:14, 15). (Cox & Hameloth, 2003-2009)

Biblical Support for the RBP

Luke 6:37: "Do not judge, and you will not be judged. Do not condemn, and you will not be condemned. Forgive, and you will be forgiven."

Matthew 6:12: "Forgive us our debts, as we also have forgiven our debtors."

Literature Support for the RBP

Because of the sin nature, man does not always behave in ways that are kind to others; therefore, the need for forgiveness and biblical discipline (RBP #10 & 5). SER emphasizes safe environments. This goes beyond just safety from fire, intruders, or other acts of violence, it also includes an environment that is psychologically and socially safe. Comer (2004) reinforced the need for a safe environment by emphasizing child development through six developmental pathways: physical, cognitive, psychological, language, social, and ethical. This emphasis on the child's development in all areas helps to ensure a safe caring environment and is encouraged through the teacher-training supplement.

Examples of How to Apply the RBP to Teaching in General

Teachers need to model giving and receiving forgiveness. When they do or say something inappropriate, they need to be willing to ask for the forgiveness of the person or group they have offended.

11— Recognize the distinctive talents that individual children possess and create an environment where they can thrive.

Define Key Terms Within the RBP

Webster (1828) defined *individual* as a "separate or distinct existence, a state of oneness." Youmans (2004) explained further,

> This principle is a revelation of the Living God's infinite and diverse nature, which He gloriously imprinted upon His whole creation (Imago Dei). God spoke the creation of the universe into existence by "the word of His power," and He maintains the integrity of each species "according to its own kind" (Gen 1:21, 24, 25). Incredibly, God created man in His own image and gave him dominion over His creation. (p. 1)

Biblical Support for the RBP

Romans 12:4-8:

> Just as each of us has one body with many members, and these members do not all have the same function, so in Christ we who are many form one body, and each member belongs to all the others. We

> have different gifts, according to the grace given us. If a man's gift is prophesying, let him use it in proportion to his[a]faith. If it is serving, let him serve; if it is teaching, let him teach; if it is encouraging, let him encourage; if it is contributing to the needs of others, let him give generously; if it is leadership, let him govern diligently; if it is showing mercy, let him do it cheerfully.

First Corinthians 12:14 & 27: "Now the body is not made up of one part but of many...Now you are the body of Christ, and each one of you is a part of it."

Literature Support for the RBP

The Hebrew for Proverbs 22:6 means, literally, "train (start) a child according to his [the child's] way." This means to train the child in keeping with their unique God-given bent, disposition, talents, and gifts. It is to consider the uniqueness of the child. "It is...for a parent to encourage, nurture, guide, and inform a child so that the child himself is prepared to choose the path that is right for him" (Wilson, 2003, p. 293). The responsibility is for the parents to study children's natural God-given personality, temperament, and creativity and direct them to fulfill their unique destiny.

Eisner (2005) advised teachers to recognize the distinctive talents that individual children possess and create an environment that actualizes those potentialities.

Examples of How to Apply the RBP to Teaching in General

Teachers can recognize the distinctive talents that individual children possess and create an environment in which they can thrive by incorporating art, music, literature, creative writing, and math in every lesson plans. Being aware of multiple intelligence helps teachers prepare lessons that respect the individuality of every child.

. . .

12— Parents need to be responsible for their children's education.

Define Key Terms Within the RBP

Webster (1828) defined *parent* as "a father or mother; he or she that produces young. The duties of parents to their children are to maintain, protect and educate them."

Biblical Support for the RBP

Deuteronomy 6:4-7:

> Hear, O Israel: The LORD our God, the LORD is one. Love the LORD your God with all your heart and with all your soul and with all your strength. These commandments that I give you today are to be upon your hearts. Impress them on your children. Talk about them when you sit at home and when you walk along the road, when you lie down and when you get up.

Ephesians 6:1-4:

> Children, obey your parents in the Lord, for this is right. "Honor your father and mother"—which is the first commandment with a promise —"that it may go well with you and that you may enjoy long life on the earth." Fathers, do not exasperate your children; instead, bring them up in the training and instruction of the Lord.

Galatians 4:1:

> What I am saying is that as long as the heir is a child, he is no different from a slave, although he owns the whole estate. He is subject to guardians and trustees until the time set by his father.

Literature Support for the RBP

Catsambis (2007) recommended specific ways parents can become involved in a positive way to support a culture of care for their children.

> Effective parental involvement includes: (a) establishing a positive learning environment at home; (b) communicating with school about educational programs and student progress; (c) participating and volunteering at school; (d) participating in students' learning at home; (e) being involved in school decision-making; and (f) collaborating with the community to increase students' learning. (para. 2)

Examples of How to Apply the RBP to Teaching in General

Teachers can demonstrate this principle by having an open-door policy for parents to participate in all classroom activities. They need to keep open communication with the parents and keep them abreast of their child's progress through phone calls, notes, and conferences.

13— Cultivate emotional intelligence—Self-awareness, self-management, social awareness, and social skills (Goleman, 1995, 2002, 2006).

Define Key Terms Within the RBP

Goleman et al. (2002) applied emotional intelligence to the position of leader in the school setting in *Primal Intelligence*. They gave some principles for building leadership through emotional intelligence that are valuable to a clear understanding of practice. Emotional intelligence is defined as a composite set of abilities that enable a person to manage themselves and others. They include:

- Self-awareness, including emotional self-awareness, accurate self-assessment, and self-confidence;
- Self-management, including achievement orientation, adaptability, initiative, trustworthiness, conscientiousness, and self-control;

- Social awareness, including empathy, service orientation, and organizational awareness;
- Social skills, including leadership, influence, communication, developing others. (Boyatzis as cited in Harris et al, 2003, p. 176)

Biblical Support for the RBP

Romans 12:9-10: "Love must be sincere. Hate what is evil; cling to what is good. Be devoted to one another in brotherly love. Honor one another above yourselves."

Romans 12:7-8:

> If it is serving, let him serve; if it is teaching, let him teach; if it is encouraging, let him encourage; if it is contributing to the needs of others, let him give generously; if it is leadership, let him govern diligently; if it is showing mercy, let him do it cheerfully.

Literature Support for the RBP

Cohen (1999) addressed the need for emotional intelligence: "Self-reflective capacities and the ability to recognize what others are thinking and feeling provide the foundation for children to understand, manage, and express the social and emotional aspects of life" (p. 10).

Building on work undertaken by the Northeast Foundation for Children and described by Charney, Crawford, and Wood (1999), Elliot (1999) identified five key dimensions that represent core attitudes and skills: cooperation, assertion, responsibility, empathy, and self-control (CARES). These skills are emphasized in order to create a climate of care where students feel free to take academic risks.

Examples of How to Apply the RBP to Teaching in General

Teachers can cultivate emotional intelligence in their students by encouraging them to try to put themselves in the place of others. This takes a lot of time and training, but it is well worth the investment of time.

14— Create an atmosphere of trust and safety.

Define Key Terms Within the RBP

Webster (1828) defined *trust* as "confidence; a reliance or resting of the mind on the integrity, veracity, justice, friendship or other sound principle of another person." Proverbs 29:25b says, "He that putteth his trust in the Lord shall be safe." Strong (1890) used the Hebrew word *batach*, which means "to trust, trust in; to have confidence, be confident; to be bold; to be secure" (#982).

Webster (1828) defined *security* as "protection; effectual defense or safety from danger of any kind...Freedom from fear or apprehension; confidence of safety." Strong (1890) used the Hebrew word *betach*, which means "security, safety" (#983). Leviticus 25:18-19 says, "'Follow my decrees and be careful to obey my laws, and you will live safely in the land. Then the land will yield its fruit, and you will eat your fill and live there in safety."

Biblical Support for the RBP

Galatians 6:2: "Carry each other's burdens, and in this way you will fulfill the law of Christ."

Psalm 22:8: "He trusts in the LORD; let the LORD rescue him. Let him deliver him, since he delights in him."

Literature Support for the RBP

Students need to know that they are valuable to God. It is important to help students feel safe and secure emotionally in order to succeed in school. Brooks (as cited in Cohen, 1999) said, "Strengthening self-esteem and...a student's sense of security and self-worth in a classroom provides the scaffolding that supports increased learning, motivation, self-discipline, realistic risk-taking, and the ability to deal effectively with mistakes" (p. 62).

Marlow (1977) suggested three ways an emotionally healthy environment can be created: "(a) unconditional love with plenty of positive reinforcement, (b) realistic discipline which holds children responsible for their actions within the limits of their abilities (RBP #5), and (c) a support system which is dependable and truthful" (p. 67).

Yount (1999) suggested four actions that help create a safe and caring environment: "(a) first, we must root out any attitudes or teacher practices that have toxic effects on students; (b) focus on personal transparency before students; (c) relate course content to the needs of students; and (d) provoke the heart" (pp. 63-64). Negative attitudes make opportunities for the practice of forgiveness, and a proper understanding of biblical discipline requires the heart attitude to be right.

Examples of How to Apply the RBP to Teaching in General

Teachers can create an atmosphere of trust and safety by paying attention to details like room set-up, access to doors, and having an emergency plan in place.

Teachers can create an atmosphere of trust and safety by being honest with students, teachers, and parents.

15— Listen to students, parents, and teachers.

Define Key Terms Within the RBP

Webster (1828) defined *listen* as "to hearken; to give ear; to attend closely with a view to hear...to obey; to yield to advice; to follow admonition."

Biblical Support for the RBP

Proverbs 4:1, 20: "Listen, my sons, to a father's instruction; pay attention and gain understanding...My son, pay attention to what I say; listen closely to my words."

Proverbs 7:24: "Now then, my sons, listen to me; pay attention to what I say."

Literature Support for the RBP

Listening skillfully nourishes others. As Brady (2003) said, "Listen with your body, your heart, your eyes, your energy, your total presence. Listen in silence, without interrupting. Fill any silence between you with love, with silent permission for the other person to go on and go deeper" (p. 15). Listening skillfully to parents, students, and teachers helps to create a community of care.

Listening is critical to the church in training children in order to pass on the faith. Seymour and Miller (1990) explained this community of believers in this way:

> It means to be with another, to claim another's joys and sorrows as our own (Rom 12:15). It means we lay ourselves open to what others are going through, and go through it with them (Hebrews 13:3). It means to care, to be there, to be vulnerable, to be compassionate. (p. 142)

Bernstein et al. (1988) researched the role of parents and supportive adults in the lives of children: "Children do best when exposed to a variety of interesting materials and experiences, but not so many that they are overwhelmed. The presence of a supportive and stimulating adult is also important" (p. 57).

Examples of How to Apply the RBP to Teaching in General

Teachers can practice listening to students, parents, and other teachers by looking directly at them when they talk, mimicking body language, rephrasing what was heard, and acting on requests whenever possible.

. . .

16— Teach through role modeling Christian virtues.

Define Key Terms Within the RBP

Webster (1828) defined *virtue* as "moral goodness; the practice of moral duties and the abstaining from vice, or a conformity of life and conversation to the moral law."

Biblical Support for the RBP

James 1:22: "Do not merely listen to the word, and so deceive yourselves. Do what it says."

Second Peter 1:5-7: "And beside this, giving all diligence, add to your faith virtue; and to virtue knowledge; and to knowledge temperance; and to temperance patience; and to patience godliness; and to godliness brotherly kindness; and to brotherly kindness charity."

Luke 6:40: "A student is not above his teacher, but everyone who is fully trained will be like his teacher."

Luke 6:45: "The good man brings good things out of the good stored up in his heart, and the evil man brings evil things out of the evil stored up in his heart. For out of the overflow of his heart his mouth speaks."

Literature Support for the RBP

Since teachers have such a pivotal role to play in nurturing the whole child, they must be men and women of the highest moral character (RBP #16). Elliot (1999) recorded a list of the desired characteristics for teachers of the 21st century, which included the following:

> (a) holds selfless love for students; (b) exhibits commitment and fairness to all; (c) treats students as whole persons; (d) models thinking and problem-solving strategies; (e) knows students' needs thoroughly; (f) is skilled at classroom management; (g) is globally-aware and visionary as a leader; (h) has the ability to manage change; (i) can set

> clear standards and hold high expectations of themselves and others; and (j) is able to work with parents and other adults. (p. 31)

Elliot (1999) further expanded what it means to teach Christianly:

> (a) The teacher who is a sincere, Bible-believing teacher will automatically teach Christianly. (b) Teaching christianly is essentially the modeling of Christian love, virtue, and morality. (c) Teaching christianly consists of devotional exercises such as prayer, Bible reading, and the singing of appropriate hymns (along with the study of Bible as a curricular subject), to be added to a standard, more or less, objective curriculum and teaching practice. (d) Teaching christianly means to imprint truth on impressionable minds. (e) Teaching christianly means to imitate the way Jesus taught. (f) The essential (sic) of teaching christianly is to impart a Christian perspective on subject matter. (p. 125)

Van Brummelen (2005) stated, "We need schools that nurture collegiality, that promote a Christian ethos, and that work toward effective Christ-centered learning" (p. 20). These concepts support RBP #16 of modeling Christian virtues.

The Hebrew culture emphasized the teacher's moral character as well as their ability to teach. The Hebrew word *lamad* (Strong's #3925) has the idea of training as well as educating or teaching by example. The Hebrew language uses one root (*lamad*) for the two words "to teach" and "to learn." In the *Theological Word Book of the Old Testament,* Vol. 1, *lamad* is one of the 12 words for teaching in the Old Testament. *Lamad* has the idea of training as well as educating. It is used this way in Deuteronomy 4:10, 5:1, 14:23, 17:19, 31:12-13 and Psalms 69:7, 71, and 73. As the teacher models Christian virtues, they are teaching by example the most important lessons of life.

Barna (2003) concluded, "A person's moral foundations are generally in place by the time they reach age nine" (para. 4). This lays a great responsibility on both parents and teachers to model Christian virtues.

Examples of How to Apply the RBP to Teaching in General

Teachers can model Christian virtues by living in close relationship with the Lord and letting His Spirit live in them. Demonstrating the fruit of the Spirit (Gal 5:20-22) is another way teachers can model Christian virtues.

17— Support fellow teachers and parents.

Define Key Terms Within the RBP

Webster (1828) defined *support* as "to bear; to sustain; to uphold...to endure without being overcome."

Biblical Support for the RBP

Galatians 6:3: "Carry each other's burdens, and in this way you will fulfill the law of Christ."

John 13:34-35: "A new command I give you: Love one another. As I have loved you, so you must love one another. By this all men will know that you are my disciples, if you love one another."

Hebrews 10:24: "And let us consider how we may spur one another on toward love and good deeds."

Literature Support for the RBP

A few examples from the literature are included by way of a representative sampling to support the need for loving relationships with God and others. A synthesis of the findings that will be applied to the Kingdom education include: relationship-focused professional development that is long-term, communities of collegial support, classroom observations, and integrated unit planning (Hameloth, 2007.

Bernstein et al. (1988) concluded,

> Children do best when exposed to a variety of interesting materials and experiences, but not so many that they are overwhelmed. The presence of a supportive and stimulating adult is also important. Children need to know that their actions have predictable consequences. (p. 57)

This goes along well with RBP #17. Support fellow teachers and parents.

Kose (2007) recommended collegial support through scheduled daily common planning and preparation time for teams to plan integrated units, discuss strategies for meeting students' needs, and share teaching methods. This supports teachers and encourages parents as their children's individual needs are met (RBP #17).

Teddlie and Reynolds (2000) recommended, "collaborative observation, teachers working together to pinpoint areas in need of improvement, teachers developing cohort (e. g., grade levels, key stages) and departmental goals for improving certain skills, and administrators and teachers establishing tailor made staff development plans" (p. 65). These ideas help create a community of care where teachers are supported in their goal of serving the parents (RBP #17).

Kinsey (2006) recommended training teachers and supporting new teachers by developing formal training programs, providing materials and support through professional development activities, and having principals meet with new teachers weekly. All these ideas are fundamental for supporting teachers (RBP #17).

Examples of How to Apply the RBP to Teaching in General

Teachers can support parents by keeping them informed of their child's progress through notes, phone calls, emails, and monthly newsletters. It is important to not just call a parent when the child is in trouble, but to find time to call to share positive news as well.

Teachers can support other teachers by sharing ideas that work well, sharing materials, cleaning up common areas, praying, and remembering special days like birthdays and anniversaries.

18— Love God and others through applying the seven governmental principles of the Principle Approach.

Define Key Terms Within the RBP

The Principle Approach is a Christian school philosophy and methodology that has demonstrated a high degree of success in building a biblical worldview in its students as measured by the PEERS test (Nehemiah Institute, 2010). The Principle Approach was developed by Rosalie J. Slater and Verna Hall as they studied the principles of God's Word. It is a biblical method of education that is designed to promote liberty to the individual and society through emphasizing a loving relationship with God and man.

The basic seven principles of the Principle Approach as revised by Rose (1992) and Youmans (2008) for an international audience are God's principle of individuality, Christian self-government, Christian character, conscience is the most sacred of all property, the biblical form of government, local self-government, and unity producing union. The principles are relationship-rich in that they help establish the true picture of man as created in the image of God.

God's principle of individuality helps students, parents, and teachers value the individuality of each other. Christian character emphasizes putting others' needs before one's own. It strengthens what is virtuous and good and helps to crucify the flesh. Christian self-government and local self-government go hand in hand to strengthen relationships through controlling impulses that destroy others through unkind words and actions. Conscience, the most sacred of all properties, helps to establish the boundaries that allow for strong relationships to develop. When people recognize the right of others to have different opinions and honor that right as their natural property, they act in a way that allows for differences without seeing them as detrimental. Government is necessary for people to live together in harmony. Protecting life, liberty, and property is the natural responsibility of the government and is necessary due to the sin nature. In I Corinthians 8, Paul speaks to Christians about guarding those new believers who have a weak conscience. Acknowledging unity out of diversity helps to strengthen relationships because each person is accepted as unique and valuable to the whole. Just as the Ten Commandments deal with our relationship with God first and then with others, so the Principle Approach begins with our relationship with God and moves on to our relationships with others; therefore, it supports the philosophy of the Kingdom curriculum.

Biblical Support for the RBP

First Corinthians 12:14 & 27: "Now the body is not made up of one part but of many...Now you are the body of Christ, and each one of you is a part of it."

Matthew 5:16: "In the same way, let your light shine before men, that they may see your good deeds and praise your Father in heaven."

Proverbs 16:32: "Better a patient man than a warrior, a man who controls his temper than one who takes a city."

First Corinthians 8:9: "Be careful, however, that the exercise of your freedom does not become a stumbling block to the weak."

First Corinthians 1:10:

> I appeal to you, brothers, in the name of our Lord Jesus Christ, that all of you agree with one another so that there may be no divisions among you and that you may be perfectly united in mind and thought.

Literature Support for the RBP

Barclay (1974) studied the Hebrew culture extensively, and many of the things they taught are exactly supported by the seven governmental principles of the Principle Approach. The Hebrew education began with the fear of the Lord and then focused on self-worth in God's kingdom. A clear understanding of the worth of each individual is based on his intrinsic value as God's own child. People are created in the image and likeness of God and, therefore, are seen as special creations of divine origin and endowment. Each child must be accepted as an individual whose worth is not dependent on what they produce. This is supported by God's principle of individuality.

Slater (1965/1999) defined God's principle of individuality, which supports this principle as "everything in God's universe is revelational of God's infinity, God's diversity, God's individuality. God created distinct individualities. God maintains the identify and individuality of every thing which He created" (p. 65).

> It is well established scientifically that all living things have within themselves a complete set of instructions for their own development and for the propagation of the next generation. All history attests to the fact that organisms have always reproduced like kinds. Furthermore, the kinds are limited by the reproducibility of their respective offspring, an axiomatic principle controlled by the chromosomes (DNA), the number and type of which are characteristic of each kind of organism. (Scott, 2000)

Examples of How to Apply the RBP to Teaching in General

God's principle of individuality. Teachers can bring this principle into all subjects as they teach about God's uniqueness in creating each thing different from all others. In math, each number is distinctively different; 3 is not 2 or any other number. Adding is not the same as subtracting or multiplying. In reading, each story is uniquely different, and each character within the story is representative of God's principle of individuality. In history, every event studied is different from the rest. Key individuals are studied in history, Bible, science, literature, etc. Teachers can also help each individual child know he or she is special to God. No two are exactly alike, but all are incredibly valuable to God. This is an RBP because it helps teachers and children value each other, which is foundational in healthy relationships.

Christian self-government. Teachers can use this principle every day to reinforce positive behavior. Children are made in the image of God and answer to Him for their individual behavior. They govern themselves based on the principles of God's Word. This is an RBP in that the way we treat others, whether positively or negatively, impacts relationships. As children learn to govern themselves with Christian self-government, they are respecting others and, thereby, strengthening healthy relationships.

Christian character. Teachers can role model Christian character and look for ways to reinforce positive character when they observe it by speaking positively and affirming the action, by writing positive notes, and by focusing on a special character trait each week or month. This is an RBP in that our character is a reflection of our personality, yet it can be shaped through our interactions with others. When one person submits their will to another person, we say he or she is demonstrating the character of deference. As teachers and children focus on Christian character, they will build stronger, healthier relationships with each other.

Conscience is the most sacred of all properties. Teachers can demonstrate this principle by being a good steward of their own materials and general school property. They can also reinforce this with the children in how they steward their property. It also goes beyond stewardship of external property and includes never forcing someone to go against their conscience. This is an RBP in that our interactions with others reveal our internal beliefs about them. For instance, if one person chooses not to participate in an activity because he or she has a weak conscience, others have the choice to accept that behavior or reject the person. Therefore, practicing tolerance and acceptance of one another of differing beliefs is a way to strengthen healthy relationships.

Local self-government. Teachers can emphasize this principle by talking about the sovereignty of God and how He is in charge of the whole universe and then remind students that parents are in charge of their own children and they delegate that authority to teachers. Each person must give an account to God for their own behavior, but we also have an obligation to try to influence others for good. That is how local self-government grows from the individual to the larger community. This is a, RBP in that one person's choice influences others. As each one governs oneself properly, one influences others around one to do the same.

Unity producing union. Teachers can demonstrate this principle by reinforcing cooperation in the classroom. As children work together, they bring unity to the school and thereby build up the body of Christ.

HOW DO I BEGIN?

Wow! Congratulations! You made it to Chapter Ten and we are almost done, but this is where there is a lot of variation depending on what school setting you are currently in. We can always start where we are and make it better. Even in the best schools, the secret of their success is continuous reevaluation and tweaking what is working to make it go from better to best.

So far, we have talked about how you start with prayer and seeking God through studying His Word. Hopefully, you have begun to synthesize some Kingdom principles you find are most important. I will be giving you some examples, but they are just suggestions. There is no codified way to teach Kingdom education that will produce exceptional results. I do have experience with the Principle Approach, so I rely heavily on that, since I saw how developing loving relationships with my students, parents and fellow-teachers created communities of care. In those conditions, students thrive. They take responsibility for their own learning and grow in their love for God and others. They are not perfect, but are on their own journey to becoming Kingdom citizens who will one day rule and reign with Christ.

The suggestions I make can be adjusted for your school year and your setting. I am going to develop it based on four quarters of approximately nine weeks each. This allows for about 45 days a quarter and results in a school year of 180 days. Again, you can start with any month and expand or delete as necessary.

One thing we did in the Principle Approach that I feel is very helpful is that each grade reviews the whole timeline and all the principles each year. This repetition is necessary for mastering the most important aspects of the curriculum. Then, each grade takes a different principle and focuses on that one. That allows you to go deeply into all the principles over the course of the school experience. For instance, everyone starts with the sovereignty of God. We use school devotional times, chapel, morning meetings, teachers' meetings, etc. to emphasize this key principle. Then one grade level will focus on it throughout the year in every subject. In history, it is easy to show the sovereignty of God in His hand of providence. In math, you show how numbers all follow predetermined rules that govern the subject. In English, you discuss the rules of grammar and how they are necessary for clear communication. Language is a gift of God and is part of the imago Dei. In science, art, music, drama, etc. you show how God sovereignly worked in the life of the key individuals you study. Hopefully, you get the idea of how this works from this brief description.

So, how do we begin developing curriculum for Kingdom education? Start with the whole year by laying out the key concepts you want to cover in a general sense first. I recommend you take a blank table and divide it into four quarters of nine weeks each and begin to put in the key concepts you feel are most important. Allow for holidays and special days to help you design your curriculum overviews.

	Quarter 1	Quarter 2	Quarter 3	Quarter 4
week 1				
week 2				
week 3				
week 4				
week 5				
week 6				
week 7				
week 8				
week 9				

Once you have the big picture, you begin to focus on units of study. A unit can take a month or just a few weeks, each one will be different, but that is how you begin. You develop the units of study. Try to incorporate wholistic learning by building unit studies that follow the guidelines established in the earlier chapters. The more ways you can stimulate the senses, the richer the learning experience and the longer it will be remembered. Incorporate music, art, drama, special days, festivals, etc. whenever possible.

Unit Overview

Topic: Botany Genesis 1:11-13

Thematic Statement: As children of God's kingdom, who have been given dominion over the earth, we need to understand botany to be good stewards of God's creation.

Objective: The goal of this unit is to help students develop a love and appreciation for the role plants have in sustaining life on earth; to help them fall deeper in love with God as the creator and sustainer of all things; to introduce them to the structure, functions, properties, habits, and arrangement of plants; and to enrich their learning through art, music, literature, and experimentation with plants.

Guiding Questions:

How do plants help our environment?

Why do you think God made plants to reproduce after their own kind?

Imagine what the world would be like without plants.

How would life on earth be different?

What responsibilities do we have for studying botany?

Why is it worth our time and effort?

Linkages with state or provincial standards: (Common Core Curriculum 4th grade Science)

CCSS.ELA-LITERACY.RI.4.2

Determine the main idea of a text and explain how it is supported by key details; summarize the text.

CCSS.ELA-LITERACY.RI.4.9

Integrate information from two texts on the same topic in order to write or speak about the subject knowledgeably.

CCSS.ELA-LITERACY.RI.4.6

Compare and contrast a firsthand and secondhand account of the same event or topic; describe the differences in focus and the information provided.

Resources:

The Bible Genesis 1:11-13

George Washington Carver Biography

Apologia Young Explorer Series: *Exploring Creation with Botany*

Plants, Seeds, Cuttings, Flowers, Microscope, Potting soil, containers, wax paper, and iron

Introductory Activity:

Have enough lima beans for each student to have two. Soak them in water overnight. Discuss the importance of a seed to reproduction. Read the Genesis passage about each plant reproducing "after his own kind" and discuss what would happen if seeds didn't reproduce after their own kind. Teach the parts of the seed and have students take notes. Then have them open the seed coat and find the endosperm and embryo.

Student Assessment:

Diagram seed and dissect the lima beans

Reason Questions

Leaf collections

Classification of leaves, seeds, and pictures of various plants

Report on a famous person from Botany

Culminating Activity:

Watch *The Secret Garden* movie. Make a homemade soup with lots of fresh vegetables from a local farmer's market or our school garden. Share with parents and community all the things we have learned about plants. Display notebooks and experiments, art work, etc.

Review the Effectiveness of your unit: Rate each objective on a scale of 1-5, 1 not very effective and 5 very effective.

Did students develop a love and appreciation for God and His creation? 1 2 3 4 5

Did students demonstrate love for God as the creator and sustainer of all things? 1 2 3 4 5

Were students introduced to the structure, functions, properties, habits and arrangement of plants? 1 2 3 4 5

Were students enriched through art, music, literature and experimentation with plants? 1 2 3 4 5

After you have created your yearly overviews and units of study, then you begin to create daily lesson plans and decide how and when you will incorporate each of the key principles: relationship building, biblical, subject, etc. There is no one lesson plan format that works for everyone. Keep it simple, but be sure you are letting the principles guide you in creating your objectives. Also remember to have authentic ways to measure student learning. This will be developed more fully in the next chapter. Here is what a completed lesson plan may look like:

LESSON PLAN

Grade: _4_ **Date: (Week 6)** **Teacher:**__________________ **Weekly Theme:** God's Principle of Individuality

Thematic Statement	**Objectives**	**Guiding Questions**
As children of God's kingdom, who have been given dominion over the earth, we need to understand botany to be good stewards of God's creation.	*Students will: Develop a love and appreciation for the role plants have in sustaining life on earth & fall deeper in love with God as the creator and sustainer of all things. Experiment with seeds and learn their parts.*	How do plants help our environment? Why do you think God made plants to reproduce after their own kind? What would happen if a lima bean produced trees?

Linkages with state or provincial standards:	**Resources:**
CCSS.ELA-LITERACY.RI.4.2 Determine the main idea of a text and explain how it is supported by key details; summarize the text. Read Genesis 1:11-13 Discuss the main idea and summarize the text. Give examples of plants reproducing "after their own kind" and discuss what would happen if they didn't.	The Bible Genesis 1:11-13 Presoaked lima bean (2 for each student) Paper towels Various seeds of all kinds for sorting
Activity:	**Student Assessment:**
Read the Genesis passage about each plant reproducing "after his own kind" and **discuss** what would happen if seeds didn't reproduce after their own kind. **Discuss** the importance of a seed to reproduction. **Teach** the parts of the seed and have students take notes. **Experiment** - have the students open the seed coat and find the endosperm and embryo. **Draw a Diagram** – Have students draw a diagram of the seed coat, endosperm, and embryo. Label each part and tell what it is designed for. **Discuss** – Talk about the wonders of God's creation and how each seed is individually different from every other seed. **Sort Seeds** – Have a table on the side with various seeds and allow students time to sort them into their own kinds. Discuss variation within kinds.	**Students will:** Read the Genesis passage and discuss the main idea, summarize, and support with details. Take notes on seeds. Dissect the seed and label its parts. Sort seeds into various kinds. Talk about the wonder of God and His creation.
Enrichment:	**Review the Effectiveness of your Lesson**

Display books on Botany from the public library. Use calendars from previous years with beautiful artwork, especially landscapes or flowers. Read: "I Wandered Lonely as a Cloud" by William Wordsworth Display Van Gogh's "Sunflowers" Have sunflower or pumpkin seeds for children to taste.	**Notes for Next Time**	Did Students: Develop a love and appreciation for the role plants have in sustaining life on earth?	1 2 3 4 5
		Express love for God as the creator and sustainer of all things?	1 2 3 4 5
		Experiment with seeds and learn their parts?	1 2 3 4 5
		Sort seeds correctly into their kinds?	1 2 3 4 5
		Read and discuss the Genesis passage?	1 2 3 4 5

WHAT SHOULD WE BE EVALUATING?

Evaluation is an integral part of learning. In order to know if your students understand and retain what you are teaching, it is necessary to evaluate their progress. We will discuss two major types of evaluation: on-going and summative assessments. The most effective teachers evaluate progress throughout the learning units. That way, they can change the delivery method, adjust the curriculum, or make other necessary changes before the unit is complete. The way we assess learning should be through many informal ways. We do not recommend simple paper pencil testing. The reason for this is that the traditional method of testing lead to the mindset that material should be memorized, tested, and forgotten. The principle of the Kingdom should be the foundation for lifelong learning. Therefore, we want to be sure the students are mastering the subject through multiple assessments throughout the learning process. An example would be asking questions during class discussions. The key is to keep track that each child has an opportunity to share, not just the most verbal or brightest students. One simple way to do this is to write every students name on a 3 by 5 card and keep these on a metal ring. Ask a question and flip through the cards and call out the student's name. For instance, "What is the key principle demonstrated in the life of

Joseph, Samantha?" You ask the question first so everyone is listening and accountable, then you call on a specific student by using the cards, not just the one who raises their hand first. This keeps everyone accountable for all the answers.

Another informal method of evaluation is using reason questions. This can be done before the lesson as a way to review previous learning or at the end of a lesson to see if mastery has been attained. Try to use higher level thinking questions that begin with "How" and "Why" more than simple factual questions like "Who" "What" and "Where" (Bloom, 1956). An example would be "Why did Jesus tell us that we should treat others the way we want to be treated?" This kind of question requires thinking and not just regurgitating facts. Another example would be, "How would the world be different if everyone practiced the golden rule?" Give students just a few minutes to write out their answers and pass them in. This will help you know who understands the basic concept and who may need some more help. Remember, we teach each individual not just a curriculum and we will be held accountable for each child in our care.

There are also many informal ways to evaluate the student's learning using book reports, projects, diagrams, notebook work, group projects, etc. The best way to evaluate learning is through many informal assessments throughout rather than a large unit test that simply measures retention of facts. Learning should be fun and exciting to your students and the way you evaluate their learning should be as authentic as possible. Planting a garden and cultivating a love for God's creation is a significant learning experience. When students dig up a bulb and see how it reproduces bulbs on either side of the original one helps them understand the reproductive system of plants more genuinely than just reading about it and completing a matching section on a paper and pencil test.

This doesn't mean that we never use pencil and paper tests. There is a place for them and they have a value in education, but we have spent so much focus on memorization and regurgitating facts that we have overused this method of evaluation. I would caution that if you must use this kind of testing, use it sparingly and try to include essay questions and higher level thinking in addition to the matching and multiple choice questions. Avoid true-false questions, as they require guessing more often than not.

One final word on evaluation: it is a necessary part of learning and living governmentally. I plan, I do, I judge. When God created the world, He planned it by saying "Let us ..."; He executed it, "and there was..."; and then He evaluated His work, "and it was good." This pattern is foundational to our teaching and should be intrinsic in all we teach. As you develop your tools of evaluation when you plan your units of study, be sure they align with your objectives and are measurable.

SAMPLE OVERVIEWS, LESSON PLANS, TEMPLATES, AND TOOLS

In this final chapter, I will give you blank forms you can use to set up your Kingdom curriculum. Feel free to modify any of the forms to fit your particular needs. I will also supply you with a sample of what a year, month, week, and daily schedule might include. This is just one idea and it is not meant to be used verbatim. Ask the Holy Spirit to guide you as you lay out the curriculum to best meet the needs of your students, parents, and teachers.

I also invite you to join our online community at B.E.S.T.- Biblical Education Support Training. We will have additional materials you can purchase, online training, support for those just beginning as well as a forum for you to collaborate with others of like mind. We are all part of the body of Christ and are committed to coming alongside and helping one another to be the best Kingdom educators we can possibly be.

Here is a brief outline of this chapter with page numbers to help you find the resources you need. I begin with the whole year, then move on to monthly overviews, unit studies, weekly schedules, and daily lesson plans. First the blank documents will be there for you to download and use, then I will give you an example of what one might look like for your reference. God bless you in your journey.

I. Blank Forms

1. Year Overview
2. Quarterly Overview
3. Unit Plan
4. Weekly Schedule
5. Daily Lesson Plans
6. T - Chart
7. Self-Evaluation Form

II. Sample Curriculum

1. Year Overview
2. Quarterly Overview
3. Unit Plan
4. Weekly Schedule
5. Daily Lesson Plans
6. Self-Evaluation Form

III. Miscellaneous Resources

1. Dr. Claudia Berry's Kingdom research
2. Excerpts from Kingdom article by William F. Cox Jr.
3. Explanation of the Principle Approach by Rosalie J. Slater
4. Key Individual Chart
5. Key Document Chart
6. T-Chart
7. Kingdom of Heaven Scriptures
8. Kingdom of God Scriptures

I. Thy Kingdom Come by Dr. Claudia Berry – Prayer Principles

BLANK YEARLY REVIEW

	Quarter 1	Quarter 2	Quarter 3	Quarter 4
week 1				
week 2				
week 3				
week 4				
week 5				
week 6				
week 7				
week 8				
week 9				

QUARTERLY PLAN

	Theme	Bible	Math	History	Science	Language	Enrichment
week 1							
week 2							
week 3							
week 4							
week 5							
week 6							
week 7							
week 8							
week 9							

Unit Overview

Topic:
Thematic Statement:
Objective:
Guiding Questions:
Linkages with state or provincial standards:
Resources
Introductory Activity
Student Assessment:
Culminating Activity:
Review the Effectiveness of your unit:

KINGDOM EDUCATION WEEKLY SCHEDULE

"But seek ye first the kingdom of God, and his righteousness; and all these things shall be added unto you."
—Matthew 6:33

Hours	Monday	Tuesday	Wednesday	Thursday	Friday
8:00-8:10 (10 min.)					
8:10-8:40 (30 min.)					
8:40-9:20 (40 min.)					
9:20-9:40 (20 min.)					
9:40-10:40 (60 min.)					
10:40-11:20 (30 min.)					
11:20-12:10 (30 min.)					
12:10-12:40 (30 mins)					
12:40-1:00 (20 min.)					
1:00-1:30 (30 min.)					
1:30-2:00 (30 min.)					
2:00-2:30 (30 min.)					

LESSON PLAN

Grade: ___ **Date:**________ **Teacher:**___________________ **Weekly Theme:** ______________________________

KEY INDIVIDUAL CHART

____

INTERNAL	EXTERNAL

Self-Evaluation

THIS WENT WELL	NEXT TIME I WILL CHANGE THIS

Kingdom Concept Chart

Mth	Kingdom Focus	Biblical Support	Relationship Building Principle	Kingdom Principle	Timeline
Sept	Fear of the Lord	Prov. 1:7; Deut. 6:2, 8:6, 17:19; Joshua 4:24; Acts 9:31	1. Love the Lord your God… 3. Depend on the Holy Spirit	Sovereignty of God	Eternity Past
Oct	Imago Dei & Dominion Mandate	Gen 1:26-28; Gen 9; Psalm 8:6; Hebrews 2:6-8	2.Love others unconditionally 4. Nurture the imago Dei qualities	God's Principle of Individuality	Creation
Nov	Kingdom of God	Matthew 6:33; Mark 1:14,15; Matthew 13:41; Ephesians 5:5	6.Use five love languages 8.Create a community of care	Unity out of our Diversity	Fall
Dec	God the Son	I John 5:20; Matthew 14:33; 16:16; Mark 1:1; Luke 1:32; 22:70	5. Discipline in love 9. Reconcile persons to God in a supportive community	Christian Self-Government	Redemption – Life and Ministry of Christ
Jan	Kingdom Living - Sermon on the Mount	Matthew 5-7	16. Teach through role modeling Christian virtues 14. Create a community of trust & security	Christian Character	Life of Christ-His Teachings
Feb	Love God & others	Deuteronomy 6:5; 7:9; 10:12; Joshua 22:5; Matthew 22:37-40	10. Forgive others & yourself 17. Support fellow teachers & parents	Servant Leadership & Suffering	Life of Christ – Suffering and sacrifice
Mar	God the Holy Spirit	I Corinthians 12:3; John 14:26; Ephesians 4:30; Luke 1:35; Acts 1:8; 2:4; 2:33, 38; 4:8; 5:32	7. Provide emotional security 15. Listen to students, parents & fellow teachers	Kingdom Power How the seed of local self-government is planted	Holy Spirit
Apr	Fruit of the Spirit	Galatians 5:22-23; Ephesians 5:9	11. Recognize the distinctive talents of each student 13. Cultivate emotional intelligence	Be Holy & Conscience is our most sacred of all property	Church
May	The Great Commission	Matthew 28: 16-20; Mark 16:15	12. Involve parents 18. Love God & others by applying the 7 governmental principles of the PA	Salt & Light	Eternity Future

Christian School Sample

Mth	Literature	History/Geography	Science	Mathematics
Sept	*The Lion, The Witch, and the Wardrobe*	Narnia and God's Kingdom	Weather	Whole Numbers "God's Principle of Individuality"
Oct	*The Magician's Nephew*	Europe & World War II	Creation & Physics	Integers "Unity our of our Diversity"
Nov	*The Horse and His Boy*	Creation/Fall/Flood	Zoology	Fractions :"Christian Self-Government"
Dec	*Prince Caspian*	Nations/History of Israel	Anatomy	Fractions "How the Seed of Local Self-Government is Planted"
Jan	*Voyage of the Dawn Treader*	New Testament History	Oceanography	Decimals "Character"
Feb	*The Silver Chair*	Ancient History	Astronomy	Fractions-Decimals-Percent "Conscience is our most sacred property"
Mar	*The Last Battle*	Modern History	Earth Science	Algebra "If you want to be great in God's kingdom, learn to be the servant of all"
Apr	*Mere Christianity*	End Times & God's Future Kingdom	Chemistry	Problem Solving "Sovereignty of God"
May	*The Screwtape Letters*	Review	Botany	Review all principles

Quarterly Plan Sample Themes

	Quarter 1	Quarter 2	Quarter 3	Quarter 4
week 1	Sovereignty of God God in Eternity Past	Unity out of our diversity	Teach through role modeling Christian virtues	Listen to students, parents & fellow teachers
week 2	Fear of the Lord	Use the five love languages	Create a community of trust and security	How the Seed of Local Self-Government is Planted
week 3	Love the Lord your God	Create a community of care	Love God & Others Life of Christ – suffering & sacrifice	Fruit of the Spirit Church life
week 4	Depend on the Holy Spirit	Jesus the Son of God Redemption – Life and Ministry of Christ	Servant Leadership & Suffering	Be Holy & Conscience is our most sacred of all property
week 5	Imago Dei & Dominion Mandate Creation	Christian Self-Government	Forgive Others & yourself	Recognize the distinctive talents of each student
week 6	God's Principle of Individuality	Discipline in love	Support fellow teachers & parents	Cultivate emotional intelligence
week 7	Love others unconditionally	Reconcile people to God in a supportive community	God the Holy Spirit	The Great Commission Eternity Future
week 8	Nurture the imago Dei qualities	Kingdom Living-the Sermon on the Mount Life & Teaching of Jesus	Kingdom Power	Love God & others by applying the 7 PA governmental principles
week 9	Kingdom of God The Fall	Christian Character	Provide Emotional security	Be Salt & Light

Quarterly Plan

	Theme	Bible	Math	History	Science	Language	Enrichment
week 1	Sovereignty of God God in Eternity Past	Genesis 1-5	Right Start Math L1-5	Biblical Timeline-Creation	Creation – Introduce Biology	Read: *The Lion, the Witch, & the Wardrobe* Author Study	Art- study pictures of God in classical art
week 2	Fear of the Lord	Genesis 6-10	Right Start Math L6-10	Fall	Begin study of human-body	*LWW* Setting	Study the artwork of Da Vinci
week 3	Love the Lord your God	Genesis 11-15	Right Start Math L11-15	Flood	Human-soul, emotions, intellect	*LWW* Plot	Worship music from different genres
week 4	Depend on the Holy Spirit	Genesis 16-20	Right Start Math L16-20	Nations	Human-spiritual being	*LWW* Theme	Study different languages
week 5	Imago Dei & Dominion Mandate Creation	Genesis 21-25	Right Start Math L21-25	Abraham	Reflect on what we have learned.	*LWW* Reason Questions	Worship dance
week 6	God's Principle of Individuality	Genesis 26-30	Right Start Math L26-30	Isaac	Begin study of Botany	*LWW* Style Allegory	Study Poetry
week 7	Love others unconditionally	Genesis 31-35	Right Start Math L31-35	Jacob	Stewardship of creation	*LWW* Sacrificial Love	Field study botanical gardens
week 8	Nurture the imago Dei qualities	Genesis 36-40	Right Start Math L36-40	Joseph	Study Key Individuals of Botany	*LWW* Character studies	Plant a class garden
week 9	Kingdom of God The Fall	Genesis 41-45	Right Start Math L41-45	Passover	Botany results of the Fall	Celebrate what we learned	Celebrate *LWW Day*

UNIT OVERVIEW

Topic: Botany Genesis 1:11-13

Thematic Statement: As children of God's kingdom, who have been given dominion over the earth, we need to understand botany to be good stewards of God's creation.

Objective: The goal of this unit is to help students develop a love and appreciation for the role plants have in sustaining life on earth; to help them fall deeper in love with God as the creator and sustainer of all things; to introduce them to the structure, functions, properties, habits, and arrangement of plants; and to enrich their learning through art, music, literature, and experimentation with plants.

Guiding Questions:

How do plants help our environment?

Why do you think God made plants to reproduce after their own kind?

Imagine what the world would be like without plants.

How would life on earth be different?

What responsibilities do we have for studying botany?

Why is it worth our time and effort?

Linkages with state or provincial standards: (Common Core Curriculum 4th grade Science)

CCSS.ELA-LITERACY.RI.4.2

Determine the main idea of a text and explain how it is supported by key details; summarize the text.

CCSS.ELA-LITERACY.RI.4.9

Integrate information from two texts on the same topic in order to write or speak about the subject knowledgeably.

CCSS.ELA-LITERACY.RI.4.6

Compare and contrast a firsthand and secondhand account of the same event or topic; describe the differences in focus and the information provided.

Resources:

The Bible Genesis 1:11-13

George Washington Carver Biography

Apologia Young Explorer Series: *Exploring Creation with Botany*

Plants, Seeds, Cuttings, Flowers, Microscope, Potting soil, containers, wax paper, and iron

Introductory Activity:

Have enough lima beans for each student to have two. Soak them in water overnight. Discuss the importance of a seed to reproduction. Read the Genesis passage about each plant reproducing "after his own kind" and discuss what would happen if seeds didn't reproduce after their own kind. Teach the parts of the seed and have students take notes. Then have them open the seed coat and find the endosperm and embryo.

Student Assessment:

Diagram seed and dissect the lima beans

Reason Questions

Leaf collections

Classification of leaves, seeds, and pictures of various plants

Report on a famous person from Botany

Culminating Activity:

Watch *The Secret Garden* movie. Make a homemade soup with lots of fresh vegetables from a local farmer's market or our school garden. Share with parents and community all the things we have learned about plants. Display notebooks and experiments, art work, etc.

Review the Effectiveness of your unit: Rate each objective on a scale of 1-5, 1 not very effective and 5 very effective.

Did students develop a love and appreciation for God and His creation? 1 2 3 4 5

Did students demonstrate love for God as the creator and sustainer of all things? 1 2 3 4 5

Were students introduced to the structure, functions, properties, habits and arrangement of plants? 1 2 3 4 5

Were students enriched through art, music, literature and experimentation with plants? 1 2 3 4 5

KINGDOM EDUCATION WEEKLY SCHEDULE SAMPLE

"But seek ye first the kingdom of God, and his righteousness; and all these things shall be added unto you." Matthew 6:33

Hours	Monday	Tuesday	Wednesday	Thursday	Friday
8:00-8:10 (10 min.)	Greeting	Greeting	Greeting	Greeting	Greeting
8:10-8:40 (30 min.)	Worship, prayer, praise & Bible story	Worship, prayer, praise & Bible story	Worship, prayer, praise & Bible story	Worship, prayer, praise & Bible story	Worship, prayer, praise & Bible story
8:40-9:20 (40 min.)	Math	Math	Math	Math	Math Games [Assessment]
9:20-9:40 (20 min.)	Snack & Recess	Snack & Recess	Snack & Recess	Snack & Recess	Snack & Recess
9:40-10:40 (60 min.)	Reading & Language Arts	Reading & Language Arts	Reading & Language Arts	Reading & Language Arts	Reading & Language Arts
10:40-11:20 (30 min.)	History	Geography	History	Geography	History
11:20-12:10 (30 min.)	Science	Science	Science	Science	Science
12:10-12:40 (30 mins)	Lunch and Recess	Lunch and Recess	Lunch and Recess	Lunch and Recess	Lunch and Recess
12:40-1:00 (20 min.)	Literature	Literature	Literature	Literature	Literature
1:00-1:30 (30 min.)	Music	Physical Education	Dance	Physical Education	Art
1:30-2:00 (30 min.)	Enrichment Activities	Enrichment Activities	Enrichment Activities	Enrichment Activities	Enrichment Activities
2:00-2:30 (30 min.)	Worship, prayer, & praise	Worship, prayer, & praise	Worship, prayer, & praise	Worship, prayer, & praise	Worship, prayer, & praise

Lesson Plan

Thematic Statement	Objectives	Guiding Questions

Linkages with state or provincial standards:	Resources:
CCSS.ELA-LITERACY.RI.4.2 Determine the main idea of a text and explain how it is supported by key details; summarize the text. Read Genesis 1:11-13 Discuss the main idea and summarize the text. Give examples of plants reproducing "after their own kind" and discuss what would happen if they didn't.	The Bible Genesis 1:11-13 Presoaked lima bean (2 for each student) Paper towels Various seeds of all kinds for sorting

Activity:	Student Assessment:
Read the Genesis passage about each plant reproducing "after his own kind" and **discuss** what would happen if seeds didn't reproduce after their own kind. **Discuss** the importance of a seed to reproduction. **Teach** the parts of the seed and have students take notes. **Experiment** - have the students open the seed coat and find the endosperm and embryo. **Draw a Diagram** – Have students draw a diagram of the seed coat, endosperm, and embryo. Label each part and tell what it is designed for. **Discuss** – Talk about the wonders of God's creation and how each seed is individually different from every other seed. **Sort Seeds** – Have a table on the side with various seeds and allow students time to sort them into their own kinds. Discuss variation within kinds.	**Students will:** Read the Genesis passage and discuss the main idea, summarize, and support with details. Take notes on seeds. Dissect the seed and label its parts. Sort seeds into various kinds. Talk about the wonder of God and His creation.

Enrichment:	Review the Effectiveness of your Lesson		
Display books on Botany from the public library. Use calendars from previous years with beautiful artwork, especially landscapes or flowers. Read: "I Wandered Lonely as a Cloud" by William Wordsworth Display Van Gogh's "Sunflowers" Have sunflower or pumpkin seeds for children to taste.	**Notes for Next Time**	Did Students: Develop a love and appreciation for the role plants have in sustaining life on earth?	1 2 3 4 5
		Express love for God as the creator and sustainer of all things?	1 2 3 4 5
		Experiment with seeds and learn their parts?	1 2 3 4 5
		Sort seeds correctly into their kinds?	1 2 3 4 5
		Read and discuss the Genesis passage?	1 2 3 4 5

Self-Evaluation

THIS WENT WELL	NEXT TIME I WILL CHANGE THIS
Children really entered into the discussion from Genesis and shared some great insights into why we need seeds to reproduce after their own kinds.	
They loved the experiment with the seeds.	
	Have extra lima bean seeds available so they can take one home and show their families what they learned.
They enjoyed the poem and wanted to write more of their own, which led to a follow up lesson.	Have books of poetry as well as botany available.
	We didn't get time to sort the seeds, so we will save this for another day.
	Children were very curious about all the new pictures and books. Maybe save this for a later lesson next time.

Dr. Claudia Berry's Kingdom Research

Definition

Kingdom of God and the Kingdom of Heaven*

The Kingdom of God has come to earth ... in the lasting takeover of the human heart by the rule of a holy God... Whenever the citizens of the Kingdom bring His light to ... the institutions of ... man... His rule is ... powerfully evident in ordinary, individual lives, in the breaking of cycles of violence and evil, in the paradoxical power of forgiveness, in the actions of those little platoons who live by the transcendent values of the Kingdom of God in the midst of the kingdoms of this world, loving their God and loving their neighbor. (Colson, as cited in Berry, 2009)

* "The kingdom does not become the kingdom of the Father until Christ, having 'put all His enemies under His feet,' including the last enemy death, 'when He hands over the kingdom to the God and Father'" (1 Cor. 15:24-28). There is triumph over death at the first resurrection (1 Cor. 15:54-55), but death, "the last enemy," is not destroyed until the end of the millennium (Rev. 20:14; Scofield, as cited in Berry, 2009, p. 1333).

Statement of Meaning

God's kingdom may be understood in terms of "reign" or "realm." Reign conveys the fact that God exerts His divine authority over His subjects/kingdom. Realm suggests "location," and God's realm is universal. God's reign extends over all things. He is universally sovereign over the nations, humankind, the angels, the dominion of darkness, and its inhabitants, and even the cosmos, individual believers, and the church. (Brand, Draper, & England, as cited in Berry, 2009)

Overarching Kingdom Hallmark

"Behold, the *kingdom of God* is within you (NKJV) ... is in your midst" Luke

Kingdom of God: Tables of Jesus's Words

Kingdom Rule and Authority: The Trinity

God the Father

The Fatherhood* "God spoke to him saying, 'I am the God of Abraham, and the God of Isaac, and the God of Jacob.' He is not the God of the dead, but of the living" Mark 12:26-27* "He is not the God of the dead but of the living; for all live to Him." Luke 20:38; Matt22:32*

"Do not call anyone on earth your father; for One is your Father, He who is in heaven." Matt 23:9*

"For God so loved the world that He gave His only begotten Son, that whoever believes in Him shall not perish, but have eternal life." John 3:16

"And the Father who sent Me, He has testified of Me." John 5:37*

"It is written in the prophets, 'and they shall all be taught of God.' Everyone who has heard and learned from the Father, comes to Me." John 6:45*

"My Father, who has given them to Me, is greater than all; and no one is able to snatch them out of the Father's hand." John 10:29*

"I go to the Father, for the Father is greater than I." John 14:28*

"There is *only* One who is good ... if you wish to enter life, keep the commandments." Matt 19:17*; Mark 19:18*; Luke 18:19*

"Jesus said, 'With people it is impossible, but not with God; for all things are possible with God.'" Mark 10:27*; Matt 19:26*; Luke 18:27*

*God the Father Revealed Through the Son**

"All things have been handed over to Me by My Father; and no one knows the Son except the Father; nor does anyone know the Father except the Son, and anyone to whom the Son wills to reveal Him." Matt 11:27*; Luke 10:22*

"Jesus said to him, "I am the way, and the truth, and the life; no one comes to the Father but through Me. But so that the world may know that I love the Father, I do exactly as the Father commanded Me." John 14:6, 31*

"The words which You gave Me I have given to them; and they received them and truly understood that I came forth from You, and they believed that You sent Me." John 17:8*

Power of God "Deliver us from evil.* For Yours is the kingdom and the power and the glory forever. Amen." Matt 6:13*

"Do not fear those who kill the body but are unable to kill the soul; but rather *fear Him who is able to destroy both soul and body* in hell." Matt 10:28*

"And looking at them Jesus said to them, "With people this is impossible, but with *God all things are possible.*" Matt 19:26*; Mark 10:27*; Luke 18:27*

"Jesus answered and said to them, "*You are mistaken, not understanding* the Scriptures nor *the power* of God." Matt 22:29*

"Jesus came up and spoke to them, saying, "All authority has been given to Me in heaven and on earth." Matt 28:18

"You will be hated by all because of My name. Yet not a hair of your head will perish." Luke 21:17-18* [ADDITIONAL: John 10:29, 17:2]*

God, the Son

Subordinate to the Father*

"All things have been handed over to Me by My Father." Luke 10:22*

"The Son can do nothing of Himself ... whatever *the Father* does, these things the Son also does in like manner. I can do nothing on My own initiative." John 5:19, 30*

"I always do the things that are pleasing to Him." John 8:29*

"I go to the Father, for the Father is greater than I." John 14:28*

[ADDITIONAL: John 5:20, 26, 36; 7:17; 8:29, 55]*

His Dual Nature*

"But so that you may know that the Son of Man has authority on earth to forgive sins"--He said to the paralytic, "Get up, pick up your bed and go home." Matt 9:6*; Mark 2:9*, 11*; Luke 5:23*, 24*

"So the Son of Man is Lord even of the Sabbath." Mark 2:28*; Luke 6:5*

"For even the Son of Man did not come to be served, but to serve, and to give His life a ransom for many." Mark 10:45*; Matt 20:28* Holman, 1981, pp. 1475, 1481

"Truly, truly, I say to you, he who believes has eternal life. I am the bread of life." John 6:47, 48*

"Then Jesus again spoke to them, saying, 'I am the Light of the world; he who follows Me will not walk in the darkness, but will have the Light of life.'" John 8:12*

"I and the Father are one." John 10:30*

"Jesus said to him, 'I am the way, and the truth, and the life; no one comes to the Father but through Me.'" John 14:6*

"My kingdom is not of this world." John 18:36*

[ADDITIONAL: Matt 21:42, 44; Mark 12:10; 12:35, 36, 37; Luke 20:41-44; 11:31-32; Matt 12:41-42; Luke 23:46; John 4:10; 5:19-24; 8:14-58; 14:7; 19:11]*

Divine, Yet Human*

"Jesus said to him, '... the Son of Man has nowhere to lay His head.'" Matt 8:20*; Luke 9:58*

"Or do you think that I cannot appeal to My Father, and He will at once put at My disposal more than twelve legions of angels?" Matt 26:53*

"Then He said to Thomas, 'Reach here with your finger, and see My hands; and reach here your hand and put it into My side; and do not be unbelieving, but believing.'" John 20:27*; Luke 24:39*

[ADDITIONAL: Matt 3:15; 26:38, 46; 26:11-12, 26:30, 42; Luke 22:42 John 12:8 Mark 14:7, 8, 9, 36; Luke 7:34; Matt 11:19; John 4:7]*

His Mission and Work*

"Come to Me, all who are weary and heavy-laden, and I will give you rest." Matt 11:28*

"For the Son of Man has come to save that which was lost." Matt 18:11*, Luke 19:10*

"The Son of Man did not come to destroy men's lives but to save them." Luke 9:56*

"My food is to do the will of Him who sent Me, and to accomplish His work." John 4:34*

"I am the door; if anyone enters through Me, he will be saved, and will go in and out and find pasture." John 10:9*

"I am the vine, you are the branches; he who abides in Me and I in him, he bears much fruit; for apart from Me you can do nothing." John 15:5*

"Therefore, Pilate said to Him, 'So You are a king?' Jesus answered, 'You say correctly that I am a king for this I have been born, and for this I have come into the world, to testify to the truth.'" John 18:37* Holman, 1981, pp. 1483-84

"So, with many other exhortations he preached the gospel to the people." Luke 3:18

[ADDITIONAL: Matt 9:37, 12:25-27, 20:28; Luke 2:49, 4:43, 5:32, 9:56, 12:50; John 5:30-36, 6:38-40, 8:12, 10:7-8, 10-11, 27-28, 11:25-26, 12:46, 14:2-13, 15:7-10, 16; 16:4, 33]*

Jesus, the Law and the Prophets

"I did not come to abolish [the Law or the Prophets] but to fulfill [them] ... until all is accomplished" Matt 5:17-18

"...whatever you want others to do for you, do...for the...this is the Law and the Prophets" Matt 7:12

"... *love* the Lord ... with all your heart ... soul ... mind. This is the great ... commandment. The second is ... love your neighbor as yourself. On these two commandments depend the whole Law and the Prophets." Matt 22:37-40

"The Law and the Prophets were proclaimed until John; since then *the gospel of the kingdom of God* is preached, and everyone is forcing his way into it. But it is easier for heaven and earth to pass away than for one stroke of a letter of the Law to fail." Luke 16:16-17

*His Betrayal and Death**

"Behold, we are going up to Jerusalem; and the Son of Man will be delivered to the chief priests and scribes, and they will condemn Him to death, and will hand Him over to the Gentiles to mock and scourge and crucify Him, and on the third day He will be raised up." Matt 20:18-19*

"Then Jesus said to them, 'You will all fall away because of Me this night, for it is written, "I will strike down the shepherd, and the sheep of the flock shall be scattered." But after I have been raised, I will go ahead of you to Galilee.'" Matt 26:31-32*

"Therefore, Jesus said, 'For a little while longer I am with you, then I go to Him who sent Me. You will seek Me, and will not find Me; and where I am, you cannot come.'" John 7:33-34*

[ADDITIONAL: Matt 12:40, Mark 14:27,28; 9-31; Matt 17:22,23; Luke 9:22, 44, 22:37; John 2:19; John 13:33, 14:19-29, 16:5, 7, 19-20]*

Note. *RELEVANCE FOR DISCIPLESHIP:* Must the disciple die too? "If anyone desires to come after Me, let him deny himself, and take up his cross and follow Me. For whoever desires to save his life will lose it, but whoever loses his life for My sake will find it" (Matt 16:24-25).

*The Church**

Jesus said the Father had revealed Him as the Christ to Simon Barjona, of whom He declared 'You are [now] Peter, and upon this rock I will build My *church*; and the gates of Hades will not overpower it.'" Matt 16: 17-18*

New Covenant

"To the disciples Jesus said, '... this is My blood of the new covenant ... poured out for many for forgiveness of sins ... I will not drink of this fruit of the vine ... until that day when I drink it new with you in My Father's Kingdom.'" Matt 26:28-29

"My kingdom is not of this world ... not of this realm ... I am a king. For this I have been born, and for this I have come into the world, to testify to the truth." John 18: 36-37

*Resurrection and Ascension**

"Jesus commanded them, saying, 'Tell the vision to no one until the Son of Man has risen from the dead.'" Matt 17:9*

"'The Son of Man is going to be delivered into the hands of men; and they will kill Him, and He will be raised on the third day.' And they were deeply grieved." Matt 17:22-23*

"No one has ascended into heaven, but He who descended from heaven: the Son of Man. As Moses lifted up the serpent in the wilderness, even so must the Son of Man be lifted up." John 3:13-14*

"Jesus said to her, 'Stop clinging to Me, for I have not yet ascended to the Father; but go to My brethren and say to them, 'I ascend to My Father and your Father, and My God and your God.'" John 20:17*

[ADDITIONAL: See God the Holy Spirit]

Note. *RELEVANCE FOR DISCIPLESHIP*: "He who believes in Me, the works that I do he will do also; and greater works than these he will do, because I go to My Father" (John 14:12). "It is to your advantage that I go away; for if I do not go away, the Helper will not come to you" (John 16:7). "You shall receive power when the Holy Spirit has come upon you" (Acts 1:8).

The Sabbath*

"For the Son of Man is Lord of the Sabbath." Matt 12:8* "Jesus said to them, "The Sabbath was made for man, and not man for the Sabbath." Mark 2:27*

"The Lord answered him and said, 'You hypocrites, does not each of you on the Sabbath untie his ox or his donkey from the stall and lead him away to water him? And this woman, a daughter of Abraham as she is, whom Satan has bound for eighteen long years, should she not have been released from this bond on the Sabbath day?'" Luke 13:15-16*

God the Holy Spirit

As Comforter*

"I will ask the Father, and He will give you another Helper, that He may be with you forever." John 14:16* Holman, 1981, pp. 1485, 1503, 1478

"But the Helper, the Holy Spirit, whom the Father will send in My name, He will teach you all things, and bring to your remembrance all that I said to you." John 14:26*

"When the Helper comes, whom I will send to you from the Father, that is the Spirit of truth who proceeds from the Father, He will testify about Me." John 15:26*

"But I tell you the truth, it is to your advantage that I go away; for if I do not go away, the Helper will not come to you; but if I go, I will send Him to you." John 16:7*

The Indwelling of the Holy Spirit*

"For it is not you who speak, but it is the Spirit of your Father who speaks in you." Matt 10:20*

"Again I say to you, that if two of you agree on earth about anything that they may ask, it shall be done for them by My Father who is in heaven." Matt 18:19*

"If you then, being evil, know how to give good gifts to your children, how much more will your heavenly Father give the Holy Spirit to those who ask Him?" Luke 11:13*

"The Holy Spirit will teach you in that very hour what you ought to say." Luke 12:12*

"It is the Spirit who gives life; the flesh profits nothing; the words that I have spoken to you are spirit and are life." John 6:63*

"He, when He comes, will convict the world concerning sin and righteousness and judgment." John 16:8*

"The Spirit of truth, comes, He will guide you into all the truth; for He will not speak on His own initiative, but whatever He hears, He will speak; and He will disclose to you what is to come." John 16:13*

"You will receive power when the Holy Spirit has come upon you; and you shall be My witnesses both in Jerusalem, and in all Judea and Samaria, and even to the remotest part of the earth." Acts 1:8* [ADDITIONAL: Luke 24:49; John 3:8, 15:26]*

Sin Against the Holy Spirit*

"Truly I say to you, all sins shall be forgiven the sons of men, and whatever blasphemies they utter; but whoever blasphemes against the Holy Spirit never has forgiveness, but is guilty of an eternal sin." Mark 3:2829; Luke 12:10; Matt 12:31-32

Law of the Kingdom Greatest Commandments.

Kingdom Governance

"He said to him, 'You shall love the Lord your God with all your heart, and with all your soul, and with all your mind.' This is the great and foremost commandment. The second is like it, 'You shall love your neighbor as yourself.' *On these two commandments depend the whole Law and the Prophets."* Matt 22:37- 40; Mark 12:29

"You know the commandments, 'Do not commit adultery, do not murder, do not steal, do not bear false witness, honor your father and mother.'" Luke 18:20; Mark 10:19

Love the Brethren.

"A new commandment I give to you, that you love one another, even as I have loved you, that you also *love one another.* By this all men will know that you are My disciples, if you have love for one another." John 13:34-35

Kingdom Ethics: Standard of Conduct Retaliation Forbidden.

"You have heard that is was said 'An eye for an eye, and a tooth for a tooth.' But I say to you, *do not resist him* who is evil; but whoever slaps you on your right cheek, turn to him the other also." Matt 5:38, 39

"But if you do not *forgive* others, then your Father will not forgive your transgressions." Matt 61:15 "Then Jesus said to him, "Put your sword back into its place; for all those who take up the sword shall perish by the sword." Matt 26:52

Love One's Enemies.

"But I say to you who hear, *love your enemies,* do good to those who hate you, bless those who curse you, pray for those who mistreat you. Whoever hits you on the cheek, offer him the other also; and whoever takes away your coat, do not withhold your shirt from him either. Give to everyone who asks of you, and whoever takes away what is yours, do not demand it back. Treat others the same way you want them to treat you." Luke 6:27-31 (Matt 5:38-48)

Kingdom Authority Dispensed

"I will give you the keys of the kingdom of heaven; and whatever you bind on earth shall have been bound in heaven, and whatever you loose on earth shall have been loosed in heaven" Matt 16: 19

"On those who have continued with Me in My trials ... I bestow a kingdom ... that you may ... sit on thrones judging the twelve tribes of Israel." Luke 22:28-30 (NKJV)

Spiritual Law of Salvation Election.*

"No one can come to Me unless the Father who sent Me draws him; and I will raise him up on the last day ... And He was saying, 'For this reason I have said to you, that no one can come to Me unless it has been granted him from the Father.'" John 6:44*, 65*

"You did not choose Me but I chose you, and appointed you that you would go and bear fruit, and that your fruit would remain, so that whatever you ask of the Father in My name He may give to you." John 15:16*

[ADDITIONAL: Matt 15:13, 20:16, 23, 22:14; Mark 10:39-40; Matt 24:22, 31, 13:20, 27; Luke 10:20, 18:7; John 17:6]*

Equal before God.*

"Go therefore and make disciples of all the nations." Matt 28:19*; Mark 16:15* "The gospel must first be preached to all the nations." Mark 13:10*

"Repentance for forgiveness of sins should be proclaimed in His name to all the nations, beginning from Jerusalem." Luke 24:47*

"I have other sheep, which are not of this fold: I must bring them also ... they shall hear My voice, and they shall become one flock *with* one shepherd." John 10:16*

Eternal Life: *Offered to All** "For God so loved the world, that He gave His only begotten Son, that whoever believes in Him shall not

perish, but have eternal life." John 3:16* "Come to Me, all who are weary and heavy-laden, and I will give you rest." Matt 11:28*

"This gospel of the kingdom shall be preached in the whole world as a testimony to all the nations, and then the end will come." Matt 24:14*

"I say to you, he who hears My word, and believes Him who sent Me, has eternal life, and does not come into judgment, but has passed out of death into life." John 5:24*

[ADDITIONAL: Matt 18:14, 22:9-10, 28:19, 9:12; Mark 16:15, 2:17; Luke 5:31-32, 13:29, 24:47; John 3:17, 4:14, 6:37, 7:37-38]*

Eternal Life*: Offered Through Jesus Christ Alone

[see above John 3:16, Matt 11:28; also Mark 2:7, John 4:14, 6:37, 7:37]* Holman, 1981, pp. 1469-70

"I am the way, and the truth, and the life; no one comes to the Father, but through Me." John 14:6*

"This is eternal life, that they may know Thee, the only true God, and Jesus Christ whom Thou has sent." John 17:3

"The good shepherd lays down his life for the sheep ... I give eternal life to them, and they shall never perish and no one shall snatch them out of My hand." John 10:11*, 28*

[ADDITIONAL: Matt 9:12-132, 11:29-30, 15:24, 18:11, 21:42, 23:37; Mark 12:10; Luke 5:32, 19:10, 9:56; John 4:14, 5:34, 39-40, 6:27, 32, 33, 35, 50-51, 54-58, 8:12, 10:9-11, 27-28, 12:47-50]*

Nature of the Kingdom

Spiritual, Unworldly

Jesus said to them, "You know that those who are recognized as rulers of the Gentiles lord it over them; and their great men exercise authority over them. But it is not this way among you, but whoever wishes to become great among you shall be your servant." Mark 10:42-43

Mysterious—Like Unto ... Vineyard laborers.

Like a vineyard owner who hired laborers; 1st hour workers grumbled when the owner paid 11th hour workers' wages equal to theirs. Matt 20:1-14

Kingdom worker, disciple, should receive provisions from their host, "laborer is worthy of his wages" Luke 10:7

"One sows, another reaps ... I sent you to reap ... others ... labored ... you have entered into their labor" John 4: 37-38

"Do not work for ... food which perishes, but for ... food which endures to eternal life ... which the Son of Man will give to you." John 6: 27

Leaven.

"The Kingdom of heaven is like leaven ... hid in three pecks of meal, until it was all leavened" Matt 13: 33; Luke 13:21

"Beware of the leaven of the Pharisees and Sadducees ... you men of little faith ... you do not understand ... the five loaves of the five thousand ... seven loaves of the four thousand and how many large baskets you took up ... I did not speak to you concerning *bread* ... beware of the leaven of the Pharisees and Sadducees." Matt 16: 6-11

"Beware of the leaven of the Pharisees, which is hypocrisy ... there is nothing ... hidden that shall not be made known." Luke 12:1; Mark 8:15-21*Holman, 1981, pp. 1470-71

A mustard seed.

"What is the kingdom of God like, and to what shall I compare it? It is like a mustard seed, which a man took and threw into his own garden; and it grew and became a tree, and the birds of the air nested in its branches." Luke 13:18-19

A dragnet. "The kingdom of heaven is like a dragnet cast into the sea, and gathering *fish* of every kind ... they

gathered the good *fish* ... but the bad they threw away. So it will be at the end of the age." Matt 13:47-49

Life in the Kingdom

The Kingdom Belongs to...

"Do not be afraid ... for your Father has chosen gladly to give you the kingdom" (NASB) ... it is your Father's good pleasure to *give* you the kingdom." Luke 12:32 (NKJV)

"Blessed are *the poor in spirit,* for theirs is the kingdom of heaven." Matt 5: 3 "Blessed are those who have been *persecuted for the sake of righteousness,* for theirs is the kingdom of heaven." Matt 5: 10

"... do not hinder [the *children*] from coming to Me; for the kingdom of heaven belongs to such as these." Matt 19: 14

To His disciples, Jesus said, "How hard it will be for those who are wealthy to enter the kingdom of God! ... They were amazed so He said again, "Children, how hard it is to enter the kingdom of God! It is easier for a camel to go through the eye of a needle than for a rich man to enter the kingdom of God" Mark 10: 23-25

Whoever keeps and teaches others the commandments "shall be called great in the kingdom of heaven"; whoever does not is "called the least in the kingdom." Matt 5: 19

"He who loves father or mother ... son or daughter *more than Me is not worthy* of Me." Matt 10:37 Righteousness which does not surpass that of "the scribes and Pharisees" will not enter the kingdom of heaven. Matt 5: 20

"... among those born of women there has not arisen *anyone* greater than John the Baptist! Yet the ... least in the kingdom is greater than he." Matt 11:11

The Kingdom Blessed ... The meek.

"*Blessed* are the gentle, for they shall inherit the earth." Matt 5:5

"Take My yoke upon you ... learn from Me, for I am gentle and humble in heart ... you shall find rest for your souls." Matt 11:29

"... whoever does not receive the Kingdom of God like a child shall not enter it *at all.*" Mark 10:15 "Whoever receives this child in My name receives Me ... whoever receives Me receives Him who sent

Me; for he who is least among you, this is the one who is great." Luke 9:48

"... let him who is the greatest among you become as the youngest, and the leader as the servant ... I am among you as the one who serves." Luke 22:26-7

The merciful.

"*Blessed* are the merciful ... they shall receive mercy." Matt 5:7

"... if you *forgive men* for their transgressions, your heavenly Father will also forgive you ... if you do not forgive ... you Father will not forgive your transgressions." Matt 6:14-15

"... go ... learn what *this* means, "I desire *compassion,* and not sacrifice," for I did not come to call the righteous, but sinners." Matt 9:13

"Woe to you, scribes and Pharisees, hypocrites! ... you tithe ... and have neglected ... *mercy* ..." Matt 23:23

"*Be merciful,* just as your Father is merciful." Luke 6:36 "... he got up and came to his father ... while he was still a long way off, his father saw him, and felt

compassion for him ... ran ... embraced him ... and kissed him." Luke 15:20

The pure in heart. "*Blessed* are the pure in heart ... they shall see God." Matt 5:8 "everyone who looks ... to lust ... has committed adultery ... already *in his heart.*" Matt 5:28 "No one can serve two masters ... either he will hate ... one and love the other." Matt 6:24 "The *good* man out of the *good* treasure of *his heart* brings forth ... *good.*" Luke 6:45; Matt 12:35

The hated, ostracized and insulted. "*Blessed* are you when men hate you ... ostracize you ... heap insults upon you, and spurn your name as evil, for the sake of the Son of Man." Luke 6:22

"... when you give a reception, invite the poor, the crippled, the lame, the blind and you will *be blessed* since they do not have the means to repay you." Luke 14:13

Scriptures: Needed for Discipleship "*It is written,* "Man shall not live on bread alone, but on every word that proceeds out of the mouth of God." Matt 4:4

"In everything, therefore, treat people the same way you want them to treat you, for this is the Law and the Prophets." Matt 7:12

He answered and said to them, "Why do you yourselves transgress the commandment of God for the sake of your tradition?" Matt 15:3

Jesus said to them, "Did you never read in the *Scriptures,* 'the stone which the builders rejected, this became the chief corner stone; this came about from the lord, and it is marvelous in our eyes'?" Matt 21:42; Mark 12:10-11; Luke 20:17

"For the Son of Man is to go just as it is written of Him; but woe to that man by whom the Son of Man is betrayed! It would have been good for that man if he had not been born." Mark 14:21; Luke 22:22

"But he said to him, 'If they do not listen to Moses and the Prophets, they will not be persuaded even if someone rises from the dead.'" Luke 16:31

Then He took the twelve aside and said to them, "Behold, we are going up to Jerusalem, and all things which are written through the prophets about the Son of Man will be accomplished." Luke 18:31

And He said to them, "O foolish men and slow of heart to believe in all that the prophets have spoken! Was it not necessary for the Christ to suffer these things and to enter into His glory? Now He said to them, "These are My words which I spoke to you while I was still with you, that all things which are written about Me in the Law of Moses and the Prophets and the Psalms must be fulfilled." Luke 24:25, 26, 44

"You search the *Scriptures* because you think that in them you have eternal life; it is these that testify about Me; For if you believed Moses, you would believe Me, for he wrote about Me. But if you do not believe his writings, how will you believe My words?" John 5:39, 46, 47

"Did not Moses give you the Law, and yet none of you carries out the Law? Why do you seek to kill Me?" John 7:19

"Even in your law it has been written that the testimony of two men is true. I am He who testifies about Myself, and the Father who sent Me testifies about Me. So Jesus was saying to those Jews who had believed Him, "If you continue in My word, then you are truly disciples of Mine; and you will know the truth, and the truth will make you free." John 8:17-18, 31-32

"You are already clean because of the word which I have spoken to you." John 15:3

"Sanctify them in the truth; Your word is truth. As You sent Me into the world, I also have sent them into the world. For their sakes I sanctify Myself, that they themselves also may be sanctified in truth." John 17:17-19

The Antagonist: Satan, Ruler of This World "The devil took Jesus to a very high mountain and showed Him all the *kingdoms* of the world and their

glory, and said to Him "All these things I will give you, if You fall down and worship me" Matt 4: 8-9 "Now judgment is upon this world; now the ruler of this world will be cast out." John 12:31 Jesus said, "I was watching Satan fall from heaven like lightning." Luke 10: 18 Jesus said, "... the tares are the sons of the evil one." Matt 13: 38

Jesus said, "the enemy who sowed [the tares] is the devil ... the tares are gathered up and burned with fire, so shall it be at the end of the age ... [and] in that place there will be weeping and gnashing of teeth." Matt 13:39-42

Jesus said, "... false prophets [will come] ... in sheep's clothing ... [who] are ravenous wolves. You will know them by their fruits ... the rotten tree bears bad fruit ... Every tree that does not bear good fruit is cut down and thrown into the fire." Matt 7: 15-20

Kingdom Rewards* and Present Hope

"... those who are persecuted for righteousness sake ... Rejoice ... great is your reward in heaven" Matt 5:10*, 12*

"Lay up for yourselves treasures in heaven, where neither moth nor rust destroys and where thieves do not break in and steal." Matt 6:20*

"For the Son of Man is going to come in the glory of His Father with His angels, and will then repay every man according to his deeds." Matt 16:27

"And Jesus said to them, "Truly I say to you, that you who have followed Me, in the regeneration when the Son of Man will sit on His glorious throne, you also shall sit upon twelve thrones, judging the twelve tribes of Israel." Matt 19:28

"His master said to him, 'Well done, good and faithful slave You were faithful with a few things, I will put you in charge of many things; enter into the joy of your master.' Then the King will say to those on His right, 'Come, you who are blessed of My Father, inherit the kingdom prepared for you from the foundation of the world." Matt 25:21,34*

"The righteous will shine ... as the sun in the kingdom of their Father." Matt 13:43*

"Do not rejoice in [your authority and power over the enemy] but that your names are recorded in heaven." Luke 10:20*

"Do not be afraid ... your Father has chosen gladly to give you the kingdom." Luke 12:32*

"Love your enemies ... do good ... lend ... expecting nothing in return; and your *reward* shall be great and you will be the sons of the Most High." Luke 6:35

"Just as My Father has granted a kingdom, I grant you that you may eat and drink at My table in My kingdom ... sit on thrones judging ... Israel." Luke 22: 29-30

"... today you shall be with Me in Paradise." Luke 23:43* "... those who did the good deeds [shall come forth] to a resurrection of life." John 5:29*

"For this is the will of My Father, that everyone who beholds the Son and believes in Him will have eternal life, and I Myself will raise him up on the last day." John 6:40

"I give eternal life to [My sheep] ... they shall never perish ... no one shall snatch them out of My hand." John 10:28*

"He who loves his life loses it, and he who hates his life in this world will keep it to life eternal. If anyone serves Me ... follow[s] Me ... where I am, there shall My servant also be." John 12: 25,26*

"In My Father's house are many dwellings ... I go to prepare a place for you ... I will come again and receive you ... that where I am ... you may be also." John 14: 2-3*

Anyone who "has left house or brothers or sisters or mother or father or children or farms, for My sake and for the gospel's sake ... will receive a hundred times as much now in the present age, houses, and brothers, and sisters and mothers and children and farms, along with persecutions; and in the age to come, eternal life ... many who are first will be last and the last, first." Mark 10:29-31

"I have not found such great faith ... in Israel ... many will come from east and west, and recline at the table with Abraham, Isaac and Jacob in the kingdom of heaven." Matt 8:11

"... when you give a reception, invite the poor, the crippled, the lame, the blind ... you will be *repaid at the resurrection* of the righteous." Luke 14:13,14

"... an hour is coming in which all who are in the tombs shall hear His voice and shall come forth ... those who did the good deed to a *resurrection of life.*" John 5:28-29*

Precepts and Principles of the Kingdom Overarching

Revelation. "Father ... You have hidden these things from the wise and intelligent and *revealed* them to infants ... no one knows the Son except the Father; nor ... the Father except the Son, and anyone to whom the Son wills to *reveal* Him." Matt 11: 25-27

Truth. "... you shall know the *truth* and the truth shall *make you free.*" John 8:32 *Sanctification.* "... everyone who commits *sin* is the slave of sin ... If therefore the Son shall

make you free, you shall be *free* indeed." John 8:34, 36 *Believe on the Lord Jesus Christ.* "... unless you *believe* that I am He, you shall die in your sins." John 8:24 *Suffering persecution:* "... because you are not of the world, but I chose you out of the world

[therefore] ... the *world hates you.*" John 15:19 *Love one another.* "A new commandment I give ... love one another ... as I have loved you ... by this all ... will know you are My disciples." John 13:34

General

Jesus summoned His twelve disciples and gave them authority [to] ... "Preach ... heal the sick, raise the dead, cleanse the lepers, cast out demons ... *freely you have received, freely give.*" Matt 10:1, 7-8

"... if two of you agree on earth about anything that they may ask, it shall be done for them by My Father ... where two or three have gathered together in My name, *there I am in their midst.*" Matt 18:19-20

"... the worker is *worthy of his support.*" Matt 10: 10

"*Grapes are not gathered from thorn bushes* nor figs from thistles, are they? ... you will *know them* ... by their fruits." Matt 16-20

"You have heard, "... love your neighbor and hate your enemy." But I say ... *love your enemies and pray for those who persecute you.*" Matt 5:43-44; Luke 6:27-28

"The *kingdom of God* does not come with observation ... the *kingdom of*

God is within you" (NKJV) ... the *kingdom of God* is in your midst." Luke 17:21

"... *seek first* His kingdom ... His righteousness; and all these things *shall be added* to you." Matt 6:33 "Therefore *do not be anxious* for tomorrow." Matt 6:34; Luke 12:31 "According to your *faith* let it be done to you." Matt 9:29 "... there is nothing covered that will not be revealed and hidden that will not be known." Matt 10:26

"... out of the heart come ...things which defile ... man." Matt 15:18, 20; Mark 7:18-23 "The *good* man out of the *good* treasure of his heart brings forth ... *good* ... the *evil* man out of the *evil*

treasure ... brings forth *evil* ... his mouth speaks from that which fills his heart." Luke 6:45; Matt 12:35 "... everyone who does evil hates the Light, and does not come to the Light for fear that his deeds will be exposed." John 3:20

Afflictions—reasons for*

"Jesus answered, "It was neither that this man sinned, nor his parents; but it was so that the works of God might be displayed in him." John 9:3*

But when Jesus heard this, He said, "This sickness is not to end in death, but for the glory of God, so that the Son of God may be glorified by it." So Jesus then said to them plainly, "Lazarus is dead, and I am glad for your sakes that I was not there, so that you may believe; but let us go to him." John 11:4*, 14-15*

"Every branch in Me that does not bear fruit, He takes away; and every branch that bears fruit, He prunes it so that it may bear more fruit." John 5:2*

Afflictions—comfort in.*

"I will not leave you as orphans; I will come to you." John 14:18* "If the world hates you, you know that it has hated Me before it hated you." John 15:18*

"Therefore you too have grief now; but I will see you again, and your heart will rejoice, and no one will take your joy away from you. These things I have spoken that you may have peace." John 16:22* Holman, 1981, p. 1460

Atonement—it was voluntary*

"I am the good shepherd; the good shepherd lays down His life for the sheep. For this reason, the Father loves Me, because I lay down My life so that I may take it again. No one has taken it away from Me, but I lay it down on My own initiative." John 10:11, 17*

Atonement—through Christ alone*

"We are going up to Jerusalem; and the Son of Man will be delivered to the chief priests and scribes, and they will condemn Him to death, and will hand Him over to the Gentiles to mock and scourge and crucify Him, and on the third day He will be raised up." Matt 20:18,19*; Mark 10:33, 34*; Luke 18:31, 33*

[ADDITIONAL: Matt 26:26-29; Mark 14:22-25; Luke 22:17-20 Mark 14:36; Luke 22:42, 23:46; John 3:13-18, 6:37-40, 51]*

Atonement—life out of death.

"Jesus said to her, "I am the resurrection and the life; he who believes in Me will live even if he dies, and everyone who lives and believes in Me will never die. Truly, truly, I say to you, unless a grain of wheat falls into the earth and dies, it remains alone; but if it dies, it bears much fruit." John 11:25-26*, 12:24*; Luke 19:19* [ADDITIONAL: John 14:19, 22, 33, 17:11-4, 19-21]*

"It is finished!" John 19:30*

Authority.*

"'What do you think, Simon? From whom do the kings of the earth collect customs or poll-tax, from their sons or from strangers?' When Peter said, 'From strangers,' Jesus said to him, 'Then the sons are exempt. However, so that we do not offend them, go to the sea and throw in a hook, and take the first fish that comes up; and when you open its mouth, you will find a shekel. Take that and give it to them for you and Me.'" Matt 17:25-27*

"Jesus perceived their malice, and said, 'Why are you testing Me, you hypocrites? Show Me the coin used for the poll-tax.' And they brought Him a denarius. And He said to them, 'Whose likeness and inscription is this?' They said to Him, 'Caesar's.' Then He said to them, 'Then render to Caesar the things that are Caesar's; and to God the things that are God's." Matt 22:18-21*; Mark 12:15-17*; Luke 20:24-25*

Backsliding.*

"But Jesus said to him, "No one, after putting his hand to the plow and looking back, is fit for the kingdom of God." Luke 9:62*

"When the unclean spirit goes out of a man, it passes through waterless places seeking rest, and does not find it. Then it says, 'I will return to my house from which I came' and when it comes, it finds it unoccupied, swept, and put in order. Then it goes and takes along with it seven other spirits more wicked than itself, and they go in and live there; and the last state of that man becomes worse than the first. That is the way it will also be with this evil generation." Matt 12:43-45*; Luke 11:24-26*

"The one on whom seed was sown on the rocky places, this is the man who hears the word and immediately receives it with joy; yet he has no firm root in himself, but is only temporary, and when affliction or persecution arises because of the word, immediately he falls away." Matt 13:20-21*; Luke 8:6,13*; Mark 4:5-6*, 16-17*

Baptism*

“But Jesus answering said to him, "Permit it at this time; for in this way it is fitting for us to fulfill all righteousness.” Matt 3:15*

“Go therefore and make disciples of all the nations, baptizing them in the name of the Father and the Son and the Holy Spirit.” Matt 28:19*

“Was the baptism of John from heaven, or from men? Answer Me." Mark 11:30*, Matt 21:25*, Luke 20:4*

“He who has believed and has been baptized shall be saved; but he who has disbelieved shall be condemned.” Mark 16:16*

“John baptized with water, but you will be baptized with the Holy Spirit not many days from now.” Acts 1:5*

Church—Christ, head of*

“You are Peter and upon this rock I will build My church; and the gates of Hades shall not overpower it. I will give you the *keys of the kingdom* of heaven; and whatever you shall bind on earth shall have been bound in heave, and what you shall loose on earth shall have been loosed in heaven.” Matt 18:18*; John 20:23*

“If two of you agree on earth about anything that they may ask, it shall be done for them by My Father who is in heaven ... where two or three have gathered together in My name, there I am in their midst” Matt 18:19-20* [ADDITIONAL: Mark 12:10, Luke 11:23; John 4:23-24 John 17:20]*

Church—unity.*

“You are the salt of the earth ... the light of the world. A city set on a hill cannot be hidden.” Matt 5:13- 14*

“Whoever does the will of My Father who is in heaven, he is My brother and sister and mother.” Matt 12:50* [12:48, 49; Mark 3:33-35; Luke 8:21]*

"Do not be afraid, little flock, for your Father has chosen gladly to give you the kingdom." Luke 12:32*

"By this all men will know that you are My disciples, if you have love for one another." John 13:35* [ADDITIONAL: Mark 13:20, 27]*

Confession—of Christ.*

"Everyone who confesses Me before men, I will also confess him before My Father who is in heaven." Matt 10:32* [Luke 12:8]*

"Whoever wishes to save his life shall lose it; but whoever loses his life for My sake and the gospel's shall save it." Mark 8:35*

Cross of Christ.*

"He who does not take his cross and follow after Me is not worthy of Me." Matt 10:38*

"And He was saying to them all, "If anyone wishes to come after Me, he must deny himself, and take up his cross daily and follow Me. For whoever wishes to save his life will lose it, but whoever loses his life for My sake, he is the one who will save it." Luke 9:23-24* [ADDITIONAL: Matt 16:24, Mark 10:21]*

Death—physical.*

"Unless a grain of wheat falls into the earth and dies, it remains by itself alone; but if it dies, it bears much fruit." John 12:24*

"The poor man dies and he was carried away by the angels to Abraham's bosom; and the rich man also died and buried." Luke 16:22 [23-31]*

Death—spiritual.*

"Do not fear those who kill the body but are unable to kill the soul; but rather fear Him who is able to destroy both soul and body in hell." Matt 10:28* [Luke 12:4-5]*

"Whoever wishes to save his life shall lose it; but whoever loses his life for My sake shall find it." Matt 16:25* [Matt 16:26; Mark 8:35-36-37; Luke 9:24-25, 17:33]*

"Unless you repent, you will all likewise perish." Luke 13:3* [ADDITONAL: John 8:51, 9:4, 12:25]*

Depravity of man.*

"You are from below, I am from above; you are of this world, I am not of this ...you shall die in your sins; for unless you believe that I am *HE*, you shall die in your sins." John 8:23-24*

"That is the Spirit of truth, whom the world cannot receive, because it does not behold Him or know Him." John 14:17* [ADDITIONAL: Matt 12:34, 15:19; John 3:19, 5:42-44, 15:24-25]*

Faithfulness*

"He who is faithful in a very little thing is faithful also in much." Luke 16:10*

"Well done, good and faithful servant; you were faithful with a few things, I will put you in charge of many things." Matt 2:21* [Matt 24:45-46]*

Forgiveness* and reconciliation.

"For if you forgive others for their transgressions, your heavenly Father will also forgive you. But if you do not forgive others, then your Father will not forgive your transgressions." Matt 6:14-15*

"Be on your guard! If your brother sins, rebuke him; and if he repents, forgive him. And if he sins against you seven times a day, and returns to you seven times, saying, 'I repent,' forgive him." Luke 17:3-4* [ADDITIONAL: Matt 5:23-26, 18:22-27, 32-35; Mark 11"25-26; Luke 12:58-59]*

Forgiveness through Christ.*

"A moneylender had two debtors: one owed five hundred denarii, and the other fifty. When they were unable to repay, he graciously forgave them both. So which of them will love him more?" Luke 7:41-42* [Luke 7:43-47]*

"Jesus was saying, 'Father, forgive them; for they do not know what they are doing.' And they cast lots, dividing up His garments among themselves." Luke 23:34*

Giving.*

"Give and it will be given to you; good measure, pressed down, shaken together, running over, they will pour into your lap. For whatever measure you deal out to *others*, it will be dealt to you in return." Luke 6:38* [Matt 5:42]*[ADDITIONAL: Matt 5:42; Mark 12:43; Acts 20:35]*

"Woe to you, scribes and Pharisees, hypocrites! For you tithe mint and dill and cumin, and have neglected the weightier provisions of the law: justice and mercy and faithfulness; but these are the things you should have done without neglecting the others." Matt 23:23*; Luke 11:42*

Hypocrisy*—decried by Jesus.

"Beware of practicing your righteousness before men to be noticed by them; otherwise you have no reward with your Father who is in heaven." Matt 6:1* [6:2, 16, 16:16]*

"Rightly did Isaiah prophesy of you hypocrites, as it is written: 'This people honors Me with their lips, but their heart is far away from Me; but in vain do they worship Me, teaching as doctrines the precepts of men.'" Mark 6:6-7*; [7:7-8, 8:15, 12:38-40]*

"He said to them, "You are those who justify yourselves in the sight of men, but God knows your hearts; for that which is highly esteemed among men is detestable in the sight of God." Luke 16:15* [ADDITIONAL: Matt 7:5, 16-20, 16:2-3, 23:5,1315, 23-30; Luke 6:46, 12:1 12:56, 11:42-53, 20:46-47; John 7:19]*

Justification.*

Pharisee and the Publican: "The tax-gatherer ... beat ... his breast saying, "God be merciful to me a sinner!... This man went ... to his house *justified* ... for he who humbles himself shall be exalted." Luke 18:14*

"He who *hears My word and believes* in Him who sent Me, *has eternal life* and *has passed out of death into life."* John 5:24*

Mysteries of the kingdom.

"To you it has been granted to know the mysteries of the kingdom of heaven, but to them it has not been granted." Matthew 13:11

Providence.*

"Are not two sparrows sold for a cent? ... not one of them will fall to the ground apart from your Father ... the very hairs of your head are all numbered" Matt 10:20-30*

"... *do not fear;* you are of more value than many sparrows." Matt 10:31*; Luke 21:18* *"Ask* and it shall be *given* to you; *seek* and you shall *find; knock* and it shall be *opened* to you. For *everyone*

who *asks receives,* and he who *seeks finds,* and to him who *knocks* it shall *be opened."* Matt 7: 7-8* "... all things for which you *pray* and *ask, believe* that you have *received* them, and they shall be *granted* you." Mark 11:24*

"Do you not ... understand ... the five loaves ... and *how many baskets you took up?* ... or the seven loaves ... and *how many large baskets you took up?* How is it that you do not understand ... I did not speak ...

concerning *bread?* ... beware of the leaven of the Pharisees and Sadducees." Matt 16:9-11*

Regeneration.*

"No one sews a patch of un-shrunk cloth on an old garment; otherwise the patch pulls away ... and a worse tear results ... [or] puts new wine into old wineskins; otherwise the wine will burst the skins, and the wine is lost ... one puts *new wine into fresh wineskins.*" Mark 2:21*; Matt 9:16-17*; Luke 5:36, 39*

"... unless one is born again ... of water and the Spirit, he cannot enter into the kingdom of God. That which is born of the *flesh* is flesh ... that which is born of the *Spirit* is spirit ... You *must* be *born again.*" John 3:3, 5, 6-7*

"If you knew the gift of God ... you would have asked Him, and He would have given you *living water* ... whoever drinks of the *water* I shall give ... [it] shall become *in* him a well of water *springing up* to eternal life." John 4:10-14*

"... he who hears My word and *believes* ... *has eternal life* and does not come into judgment but has passed out of death into life." John 5:24*

"I am the *light of the world*; he who follows Me ... shall have the light of life." John 8:12* "... to all whom Thou has given Him, He may *give eternal life.*" John 17:2*

Repentance.*

Parable of the Two Sons: Tax collectors and harlots "will get into the kingdom of God" before the disobedient and before the unbelieving. Matt 21:28-32*

"The time is fulfilled and the kingdom of God is at hand; *repent and believe* in the gospel." Mark 1:15**Holman, 1981, pp. 1497-98

"It is not...[the]...healthy who need a physician but...[the]... sick; I did not come to call the righteous, but *sinners.*" Mark 2:17*

"... unless you *repent,* you will all likewise *perish."* Luke 13:3* Parable of the Lost Sheep: "There is more joy in heaven over one sinner who *repents* than over ninety-nine

righteous persons who need no repentance." Luke 15:4-7*; Matt 18-14* Parable of the Lost Coin: "... there is joy in the presence of the angels of God over one sinner who

repents." Luke 15:8-10* Parable of the Prodigal Son: "... this brother of yours was dead and *has begun to live,* and *was lost* and has

been found." Luke 15:11-32* Pharisee and the Publican: "I tell you, this man [publican] went ... to his house justified ... for he who

humbles himself shall be exalted." Luke 18:14* "... *unless you believe that I am He,* you shall die in your sins." John 8:24*

Reproof.*

"*Woe* to you, Chorazin! *Woe* to you, Bethsaida! For if the *miracles* had occurred in Tyre and Sidon which occurred in you, they would have repented long ago in sackcloth and ashes." Matt 11:21* [Jesus ministered in all four cities but apparently performed greater miracles in Chorazin and Bethsaida]

"You, Capernaum ... shall descend to Hades; for if the *miracles* had occurred in Sodom which occurred in you, it would have remained to this day ... is hall be more tolerable for ... Sodom in the day of judgment, than for you." Matt 11:23-24*

Riches.*

"Do not store up for yourselves treasures on earth, where moth and rust destroy, and where thieves break in and steal. But store up for yourselves treasures in heaven, where neither moth nor rust destroys, and where thieves do not break in or steal; for where your treasure is, there your heart will be also. But seek first His kingdom and His righteousness, and all these things will be added to you." Matt 6:19-21*, 33

"And the one on whom seed was sown among the thorns, this is the man who hears the word, and the worry of the world and the deceitfulness of wealth choke the word, and it becomes unfruitful." Matt 13:22* (Mk. 4:7,18,19; Luke 8:8,14)*

"For what will it profit a man if he gains the whole world and forfeits his soul? Or what will a man give in exchange for his soul?" Matt 16:26*

"And Jesus said to His disciples ... it is hard for a rich man to enter the kingdom of heaven. Again I say to you, it is easier for a camel to go through the eye of a needle, than for a rich man to enter the kingdom of God." Matt 19:23-24*

"And Jesus, looking around, said to His disciples, "How hard it will be for those who are wealthy to enter the kingdom of God! The disciples were amazed at His words. But Jesus answered again and said to them, "Children, how hard it is to enter the kingdom of God!" Mark 10:23-24*

"Truly I say to you, this poor widow put in more than all the contributors to the treasury; for they all put in out of their surplus, but she, out of her poverty, put in all she owned, all she had to live on." Mark 12:43- 44*

"But woe to you who are rich, for you are receiving your comfort in full." Luke 6:24*

"And I will say to my soul, "Soul, you have many goods laid up for many years to come; take your ease, eat, drink and be merry. But God said to him, 'You fool! This very night your soul is required of you; and now who will own what you have prepared?' So is the man who stores up treasure for himself, and is not rich toward God." Luke 12:19-21*

"Do not work for the food which perishes, but for the food which endures to eternal life, which the Son of Man will give to you, for on Him the Father, God, has set His seal." John 6:27*

Righteousness.*

"... it is fitting for us to fulfill all righteousness." Matt 3:15

"Then Jesus said to him, "Go, Satan! For it is written, 'You shall worship the Lord your God, and serve Him only.'" Matt 4:10

"... unless your righteousness surpasses that of the scribes and Pharisees, you will not enter the kingdom of heaven." Matt 5:20

"But seek first His kingdom and His righteousness, and all these things will be added to you." Matt 6:33

"Then the righteous will shine forth as the sun in the kingdom of their Father. He who has ears, let him hear." Matt 13:43

"And He summoned the crowd with His disciples, and said to them, "If anyone wishes to come after Me, he must deny himself, and take up his cross and follow Me ... whoever wishes to save his life will lose it, but whoever loses his life for My sake and the gospel's will save it." Mark 8:34-35

"For God so loved the world, that He gave His only begotten Son, that whoever believes in Him shall not perish, but have eternal life. For God did not send the Son into the world to judge the world, but that the world might be saved through Him." John 3:16-17

"He who believes in Him is not judged; he who does not believe has been judged already, because he has not believed in the name of the only begotten Son of God." John 3:18

"This is the judgment, that the Light has come into the world, and men loved the darkness rather than the Light, for their deeds were evil." John 3:19

"But he who practices the truth comes to the Light, so that his deeds may be manifested as having been wrought in God." John 3:21

"... he who hears My word, and believes Him who sent Me, has eternal life, and does not come into judgment, but has passed out of death into life." John 5:24

"And He, when He comes, will convict the world concerning ... righteousness ... because I go to the Father and you no longer see Me." John 16:10

Seeking God.*

"Ask, and it will be given to you; seek, and you will find; knock, and it will be opened to you. For everyone who asks receives, and he who seeks finds, and to him who knocks it will be opened." Matt 7-8*; Luke 11:9-10*

"And do not seek what you will eat and what you will drink, and do not keep worrying. For all these things the nations of the world eagerly seek; but your Father knows that you need these things. But seek His kingdom, and these things will be added to you. Do not be afraid, little flock, for your Father has chosen gladly to give you the kingdom." Luke 12:29-32*

Self-denial.*

"The foxes have holes and the birds of the air have nests, but the Son of Man has nowhere to lay His head." Matt 8:20*

"He who loves father or mother more than Me is not worthy of Me; and he who loves son or daughter more than Me is not worthy of Me. And he who does not take his cross and follow after Me is not worthy of Me." Matt 10:37-38*

"If anyone wishes to come after Me, he must deny himself, and take up his cross and follow Me. For whoever wishes to save his life will lose it; but whoever loses his life for My sake will find it." Matt 16:24-25*; Luke 9:23-24*

"If anyone comes to Me, and does not hate his own father and mother and wife and children and brothers and sisters, yes, and even his own life, he cannot be My disciple." Luke 14:26*

"Truly I say to you, this poor widow put in more than all of them; for they all out of their surplus put into the offering; but she out of her poverty put in all that she had to live on." Luke 21:3-4*: Mark 12:43-44*

"For I have come down from heaven, not to do My own will, but the will of Him who sent Me." John 6:38*

Sin of covetousness.

"Do not lay up for yourselves treasures upon earth where moth and rust destroy and where thieves break in and steal." Matt 6:19

"Beware and be on your guard against every form of greed; for not *even* when one has an abundance does his life consist of his possessions." Luke 12:15 [ADDITIONAL: Mark 10:23; John 6:27; Mark 7:21-22]

Sin of denying Christ.

"Whoever is ashamed of Me and My words in this adulterous and sinful generation, the Son of Man will also be ashamed of him when He comes." Mark 8:38

[ADDITIONAL: Luke 9:26, 12:8-9, 22:34; Matt 26:34; Mark 14:30]

Sin of self-righteousness.

He said to them, "You are those who justify yourselves in the sight of men, but God knows your hearts; for that which is highly esteemed among men is detestable in the sight of God." Luke 16:15

The Pharisee stood and was praying this to himself: 'God, I thank You that I am not like other people: swindlers, unjust, adulterers, or even like this tax collector. 'I fast twice a week; I pay tithes of all that I get.'

Luke 18:11-12; 11:42 [ADDITIONAL: Matt 5:20, 7:22-23, 16:6, Mark 8:15, Matt 21:31-32, 23:27-31]

Sin separates from God.*

And then I will declare to them, 'I never knew you; DEPART FROM ME, YOU WHO PRACTICE LAWLESSNESS.' Matt 7:23*

"But if you do not forgive, neither will your Father who is in heaven forgive your transgressions." Mark 11:26* [ADDITIONAL: Matt 6:5; Luke 13:25]*

Sin—consequences.

"He answered and said, "Every plant which My heavenly Father did not plant shall be rooted up." Matt 15:13

"It would be better for him if a millstone were hung around his neck and he were thrown into the sea, than that he would cause one of these little ones to stumble." Luke 17:2

[ADDITIONAL: Matt 19, 18:7, 23:33, 24:51, 25:46; Luke 12:5, 19:27, 20:18, 23:30, John 5:29, 8:21] [SEE "JUDGMENT DAY—PUNISHMENT" below]

Sowing and reaping.

"The kingdom of heaven may be compared to a man who sowed good seed in his field." Matt 13:24

"The one on whom seed was sown on the good soil, this is the man who hears the word and understands it ... bears fruit and brings forth, some a hundredfold, some sixty, and some thirty." Matt 13:24

Sorrow.*

"Blessed are those who mourn, for they shall be comforted." Matt 5:4*
"Do not let your heart be troubled; believe in God, believe also in Me." John 14:1*

"Peace I leave with you; My peace I give to you; not as the world gives do I give to you Do not let your heart be troubled, nor let it be fearful." John 14:27* [ADDITIONAL: Matt 24:7, 26:38-42; Mark 14:34,36; Luke 22:42; Mark 13:18-19; Luke 23:28]*

Soul of man.*

"Do not fear those who kill the body but are unable to kill the soul; but rather fear Him who is able to destroy both soul and body in hell." Matt 10:28*

"For what is a man profited if he gains the whole world, and loses or forfeits himself?" Luke 9:25* [ADDITIONAL: Matt 16:26; Luke 20:36]** Holman, 1981, pp. 1506-07

Spiritual blindness*—warnings.

"But if your eye is bad, your whole body will be full of darkness. If then the light that is in you is darkness, how great is the darkness!" Matt 6:23*

"When anyone hears the word of the kingdom and does not understand it, the evil one comes and snatches away what has been sown in his heart. This is the one on whom seed was sown beside the road." Matt 13:19*; Mark 4:15*; Luke 8:12* [ADDITIONAL: Matt 15:14, 16:3, 22:29, 23:24; Luke 11:52, 12:48, 19:42, 23:34; John 3:7, 19, 4:10, 7:28, 8:15, 14:17, 16:3, 17:25]*

Stealing.*

"And He said to him, "Why are you asking Me about what is good? There is only One who is good; but if you wish to enter into life, keep the commandments. Then he said to Him, "Which ones?" Jesus said, "You shall not ... steal; you shall not bear false witness." Matt 19:17-18*

"For from within, out of the heart of men, proceed ... thefts." Mark 7:21*

"But store up for yourselves treasures in heaven ... where thieves do not break in or steal." Matt 6:20* [ADDITIONAL: Mark 10:19; Luke 18:20; Matt 15:19]*

Strife.*

"If your brother sins go and show him his fault in private; if he listens to you, you have won your brother." Matt 18:15*

"While you are going with your opponent to appear before the magistrate, on your way there make an effort to settle with him, so that he may not drag you before the judge, and the judge turn you over to the officer, and the officer throw you into prison." Luke 12:58* [ADDITIONAL: Matt 5:25, 39; 12:25]*

Tribulation.*

"He has no firm root in himself, but is only temporary, and when affliction or persecution arises because of the word, immediately he falls away." Matt 13:21*

"These things I have spoken to you, so that in Me you may have peace. In the world you have tribulation, but take courage; I have overcome the world." John 16:33*

[ADDITIONAL: Matt 24:15, 16, 21]*

Unity—intercessory prayer.

Jesus prayed, "That they may all be one; even as Thou Father, art in Me, and I in Thee, that they also may be in Us; ... the glory ... Thou hast given Me I have given to them that they may be one, just as We are one. I in them and Thou in Me, that that may be *perfected in unity*, that the world may know ... Father I desire that they ... be with Me." John 17: 21-24

"I was hungry ... you gave Me something to eat ... thirsty ... you gave me drink ... a stranger and you invited Me in... the King will say... *"...to the extent you did to...the least...you did it to Me."* Matt 25:35

"*Love* your enemies ... do good ... lend ... expecting nothing in return." Luke 6:35*Holman, 1981, pp. 1507-09

"Greater *love* has no one than this, that one lay down his life for his friends ...This I command you, that you love one another." John 15:13, 17

"A pupil is not above his teacher ... everyone after he has been fully trained, will be like his teacher." Luke 6:40

"... the *seed* ... among the thorns ... are ... they [who] are choked with worries ... riches ... pleasures of this life." Luke 8:14

"The Pharisee ... was praying to himself, "God I thank Thee ... I fast ... I pay tithes" ... The tax- gatherer was beating his breast, saying "God, be merciful to me, the sinner!" ... This man went down to his house *justified* rather than [the Pharisee]." Luke 18:10-13

Those who have *given up much,* "shall *receive a hundred times* as much now in the present age ... *with persecutions,* and in the age to come eternal life." Mark 10:30

"... do not be called Rabbi ... do not call anyone on earth your father ... do not be called leaders ... But the *greatest* ... shall be your *servant.*" Matt 23:8-11; Mark 10:43-44

"If anyone wants to be *first,* he shall be *last and servant of all."* Mark 9:35 "*Beware* of the scribes who *like* ... long robes ... respectful greeting ... chief seats ... and places of

honor." Mark 12:38-39; Luke 20:46

Warfare—kingdom.

"Then Jesus said ... 'Go, Satan! For it is written, "you shall worship the lord your God, and serve him only."'" Matt 4:10

"If Satan casts out Satan, he is divided against himself; how then will his kingdom stand?" Matt 12:26

"If I by Beelzebub I cast out demons, by whom do your sons cast them out? For this reason they will be your judges. But if I cast out demons by the Spirit of God, then the kingdom of God has come upon you." Matt 12:27-28; Mark 3:23-25; Luke 11:18-20

"But He turned and said to Peter, 'Get behind Me, Satan! You are a stumbling block to Me; for you are not setting your mind on God's interests, but man's.'" Matt 16:23; Mark 8:33

"These are the ones who are beside the road where the word is sown; and when they hear, immediately Satan comes and takes away the word which has been sown in them." Mark 4:15; Matt 13:19

"Simon, Simon, behold, Satan has demanded permission to sift you like wheat; but I have prayed for you, that your faith may not fail; and you, when once you have turned again, strengthen your brothers." Luke 22:31-32

"You are of your father the devil, and you want to do the desires of your father He was a murderer from the beginning, and does not stand in the truth because there is no truth in him Whenever he speaks a lie, he speaks from his own nature, for he is a liar and the father of lies." John 8:44

"Now judgment is upon this world; now the ruler of this world will be cast out." John 12:31

"I will not speak much more with you, for the ruler of the world is coming, and he has nothing in Me." John 14:30

Coming of the Kingdom

"You will ... [hear] of wars and rumors of wars; see that you are not frightened ... nation will rise against nation and kingdom against kingdom ... these ... are the beginning of birth pangs ... you will be hated of all nations on account of My name ... many will fall away and will betray one another and hate one another ... most people's love will grow cold ... the one who endures to the end shall be saved." Matt 24: 6-13*; Mark 13:7-9*

"... this gospel of the Kingdom shall be preached in the whole world for a witness to all the nations, and then the end shall come." Matt 24:14

"The gospel must first be preached to all nations ... do not be anxious ... [about] what you are to say ... [it] will be given you in that hour." Mark 13: 10-11*

The kingdom may be compared to 10 virgins—5 foolish took lamps but no oil and 5 wise who took lamps and oil. The bridegroom came unexpectedly, received those who were ready, and shut the door on the unprepared. "Be on the alert ... you do not know the day nor hour [of His coming]." Matt 25: 1-13*

"... hereafter you shall see the Son of Man sitting at the right hand of Power, and coming on the clouds of heaven." Matt 26:64*; Mark 14:62*; Luke 22:69*

Be dressed and ready, your lamps lighted ... open the door immediately when the Master comes ... the Son of Man will come at a most *unexpected* hour ... Those who knew the master's will but was not *prepared* will be assigned a place "with the unbelievers"; the one who did not know will receive more mercy. Luke 12: 35-46*

As in the days of Noah ... the days of Lot, they were drinking, buying, selling, planting, building ... [until] the day Lot went out ... judgment fell. It will be the same "on the day ... the Son of Man is revealed" Luke 17:24*

Do not be misled, many will say "I am He." Luke 21:8-9*

"Before all these things, they will ... persecute you, deliver ... you to the synagogues and prisons, bring ... you before kings and governors for My name's sake." Luke 21:12

Be on your guard that your heart is not burdened with dissipation, drunkenness, worries of life and that Day come suddenly as a trap. Luke 21:34* (vv. 10-33)*

To Nathaniel, as Jesus opened His ministry with great power, He said: *... you will see the heavens opened and the angels of God ascending and descending on the Son of Man.* John 1:51*

God's Angels*

Angels will gather out of His kingdom all stumbling blocks and lawbreakers. Matt 13:39-41**Holman, 1981, pp. 1476, 1460

"The kingdom of heaven is like a dragnet cast into the sea, and gathering *fish* of every kind ... they gathered the good *fish* ... but the bad they threw away. So it will be at the end of the age; the *angels* will come forth and take out the wicked from among the righteous and will throw them into the furnace of fire; in that place there will be weeping and gnashing of teeth." Matt 13:47-49

Angels assigned to the "little ones" are ever before the Father's face in heaven. Matt 18:10

With a great trumpet the angels will gather the elect from everywhere on the day of the Lord's return to earth, a day known only to the Father. Matt 24:31, 36

Angels will come with the Son when He comes in His glory. Matt 25:31 If the Son had requested, the Father would have sent 12 legions of angels for His defense (a legion = 6,000 troops: Scofield, as cited in Berry, 2009). Matt 26:53

Angels will witness the Believers' confession of Jesus and His confession or denial of them. Luke 12: 8-9;

Luke 9:26; Mark 8:38 Repentance of one sinner causes great rejoicing among God's angels. Luke 15:10

Angels carried the poor man after death to Abraham's bosom ; the rich man died and was buried. Luke 16:22

Jesus told Nathaniel, His disciple, he would see the heavens open and angels traversing upon the Son of Man. John 1:51

The Harvest

"Seeing the people, He felt compassion ... they were distressed and dispirited like sheep without a shepherd. He said to his disciples, "The harvest is plentiful, but the workers are few. Therefore beseech the Lord of the harvest to send out workers into His harvest." Matt 9:36-38

"Go to the lost sheep of the house of Israel...preach... "The kingdom of heaven is at hand" ... Heal the sick, raise the dead, cleanse the lepers, cast out demons. Freely you received, freely give. Do not acquire [things] ... for your journey ... for the worker is worthy of his support ... whatever city or village you enter, inquire who is worthy ... and stay at his house." Matt 10:6-11

"I send you out as sheep in the midst of wolves; so be shrewd as serpents and innocent as doves." Matt 10:16

*Kingdom Rewards and the Judgment**

"And Jesus said to them, "Truly I say to you, that you who have followed Me, in the regeneration when the Son of Man will sit on His glorious throne, you also shall sit upon twelve thrones, judging the twelve tribes of Israel." Matt 19:28

"His master said to him, 'Well done, good and faithful slave You were faithful with a few things, I will put you in charge of many things; enter into the joy of your master.' Then the King will say to those on His right, 'Come, you who are blessed of My Father, inherit the kingdom prepared for you from the foundation of the world." Matt 25:21,34

"The righteous will shine ... as the sun in the kingdom of their Father." Matt 13:*Holman, 1981, pp. 1460, 1486

"Just as My Father has granted a kingdom, I grant you that you may eat and drink at My table in My kingdom ... sit on thrones judging ... Israel." Luke 22: 29-30

"... today you shall be with Me in Paradise." Luke 23:43 "... an hour is coming in which all who are in the tombs shall hear His voice and shall come forth ...

those who did the good deed to a *resurrection of life.*" John 5:28-29 "He who loves his life loses it, and he who hates his life in this world will keep it to life eternal. If anyone

serves Me ... follow[s] Me ... where I am, there shall My servant also be." John 12: 25,26

"In My Father's house are many dwellings ... I go to prepare a place for you ... I will come again and receive you ... that where I am ... you may be also." John 14: 2-3

"I have not found such great faith ... in Israel ... many will come from east and west, and recline at the table with Abraham, Isaac and Jacob in the kingdom of heaven." Matt 8:11

"... an hour is coming in which all who are in the tombs shall hear His voice and shall come forth ... those who did the good deed to a *resurrection of life.*" John 5:28-29

Expectations Associated with Judgment Day

"... it will be more tolerable for Tyre and Sidon in the day of judgment than for you [cities where miracles were done] ... And you, Capernaum, will not be exalted to heaven ... you will descend to Hades; for if the *miracles* had occurred in Sodom which occurred in you, it would have remained to this day. It will be more tolerable for ... Sodom in the day of judgment than for you." Matt 11:22-24

"... the last shall be first, and first last." Matt 20:16; 19:30; Mark 10:31

Accountability.

Parable of the Talents: "... you ought to have put my money in the bank and on my arrival I would have received my money back with interest." Matt 25:27) [Matt 25:14-30]

"If I had not come and spoken to them, they would not have sin, but now they have no excuse for their sin" John 15:22

"... woe to you Pharisees! For you pay tithe of ... every kind ... and *yet disregard justice and the love of God."* Luke 11:42

"Woe to the world because of *its* stumbling blocks! For it is inevitable that stumbling blocks come; but woe to that man through whom the stumbling block comes!" Matt 18:7; Mark 9:42

"He who has *believed* and been *baptized* shall be saved." Mark 16:16 "He who has ... *disbelieved* shall be condemned." Mark 16:16 *Judgment Day of the Lord*

False profession. "Many will say to Me on that day, 'Lord, Lord, did we not prophesy ... cast out demons ... perform many miracles in Your name? And then I will declare to them 'I never knew you; Depart from Me, you who practice lawlessness." Matt 7: 22-23 [see delayed judgment Luke 13: 6]

Rejecting Jesus.

Parable of the Landowner: "The builders rejected the chief cornerstone ... the Lord's doing ... Therefore I say to you, the kingdom of God will be taken from you and given to a nation bearing the fruits of it." Matt 21:43 [Matt 21: 33-44]

"He who has ... disbelieved shall be *condemned*." Mark 16:16 "Once the head of the house gets up and shuts the door, and you begin ... saying ... "Lord open up to us!" ... He will answer... "I do not know...you...depart from Me." Luke13:25-27

"He who *does not believe* has been judged already, because he has not believed in the name of only begotten Son of God." John 3:18

Jews rejecting Jesus.

"The sons of the kingdom will be cast out into the outer darkness; in that place there will be weeping and gnashing of teeth." Matt 8: 12

Separation of the righteous and unrighteous.

"When the Son of Man comes … and all the angels with Him ... He will sit on His ... throne. And all the nations will be gathered before Him ... He will separate them ... as the shepherd separates the sheep from the goats ... the King will say to [His sheep], "Come ... inherit the *kingdom* prepared for you ... He will ... say to [the goats], "Depart from Me." Matt 25:31-41

"The master of that slave will come ... when he does not expect him ... and will assign him a place with the unbelievers." Luke 12:46

The Judgment. "This is the judgment, that the light is come into the world and men loved the darkness rather than the light ... everyone who does evil hates the light ... But he who practices the truth comes to the light." John 3:19-21

"And concerning judgment, because the ruler of this world has been judged." John 16:11 *At the last day.* "The word I spoke is what will judge [the one who rejects Me]" John 12:48

Punishment*

"... unless your righteousness surpasses that of the scribes and Pharisees, you shall not enter the kingdom of heaven." Matt 5:20*

"... everyone who is angry with his brother shall be guilty before the court ... whoever shall say to his brother, "Raca" shall be guilty before the supreme court ... whoever shall say, "You fool," shall be guilty enough to go into the hell of fire." Matt 5:21-11*

"Every tree that does not bear good fruit is cut down and thrown into the fire." Matt 7:19*

"Do not fear those who kill the body ... fear Him who is able to destroy both soul and body in hell." Matt 10:29*; Luke 12:5

"... as the tares are gathered up and burned with fire, so shall it be at the end of the age." Matt 13:40*

"... angels will gather out of His kingdom all stumbling blocks and those who commit lawlessness and ... will cast them into the furnace of fire ... there shall be weeping and gnashing of teeth." Matt 13:41-42*Holman, 1981, p. 1497

"... angels shall ... take out the wicked from among the righteous, and will cast them into the furnace of fire, there shall be weeping and gnashing of teeth." Matt 13:49-50

"You serpents, you brood of vipers, how shall you escape *the sentence* of hell?" Matt 23:33

"Then He will also say to those on His left, "Depart from Me, accursed ones, into the eternal fire which has been prepared for the devil and his angels ... these will go away into *eternal punishment*." Matt 25:41;46

"Whoever blasphemes against the Holy Spirit never has forgiveness but is guilty of an *eternal sin.*" Mark 3:29

"The master of that slave will come ... when he does not expect him ... and will *cut him in pieces.*" Luke 12:46

"There will be weeping and gnashing of teeth ... when you see ... yourselves being *cast out.*" Luke 13:28 "... in Hades he lifted ... his eyes ... and saw Abraham ... and Lazarus ... and he cried out ... "Father

Abraham, have mercy on me ... *I am in agony* in this flame.'" Luke 16:23-24 "... an hour is coming in which all who are in the tombs shall hear His voice and shall come forth ... those who committed ... evil deeds to a resurrection of judgment." John 5:28-29*Holman, 1981, p. 1497

DR. COX'S RESEARCH ON KINGDOM EDUCATION

If you are interested in a deeper study of Kingdom education, I highly recommend the research and writings of William F. Cox, Jr., Ph.D. He was my mentor at Regent University for many years and I owe a debt of gratitude I could never repay to him for sharing his wisdom and passion for finding a better way to educate for Kingdom discipleship. Here are a few quotes from an article used in the Christian Education program he founded and chairs. I submit it as a sampling of his writing and what you can glean if you purchase access to his articles. I also have included a sampling of some of his latest articles for you to pursue further.

Sonship

> This concept of son-ship is laden with implications for self-identity. Children of King Jesus carry all the qualities of royalty of the highest order. They are, for instance, royalty (1 Pet 2:9), citizens of a holy nation (1 Pet 2:9), official representatives of Him (2 Cor 5:20). All this likely being unfamiliar territory, students need to be taught and infused with this identity. At the same time they also need to be prepared for suffering (Phil

3:10), to accept persecution joyfully (Matt 5:10-12; John 21:18-19; 1 Pet 4:12; 1 Thessalonians 5:16-18; James 1:2) and to be ready to die ungrudgingly for their King (Rev 12:11c). Thus Christian education should help reinforce students' identity as, for example, that they are saints (Eph 1:18), accepted in the Beloved (Eph 1:6), blameless before God (Eph 1:4), chosen (John 15:19), and heirs to the throne (Rev 3:21) whose primary citizenship and final home is not this temporal world.

Relationship Education

Not a God who leaves His people without essential guidance, the reality is that He has very amply provided the understandings for quality educational prescriptions. Pointing us in that direction are various accounts (e.g., Collins & Tamarkia; Comer; Cox; Ornish, as cited in Berry, 2009) documenting that the most important understanding about education is that it is a relationship-embedded endeavor. As Comer repeatedly declared, the reason for his huge success as an educator is captured in three words – "it's all about relationship, relationship, relationship" (as cited in Berry, 2009). And as Collins similarly explained her success in teaching disadvantaged children: "The one thing all children finally wanted was the chance to be accepted for themselves, to feel some self-worth. Once they felt it, children became addicted to learning, and they had the desire to learn forever "(Collins & Tamarkin, as cited in Berry, 2009). Relationally based authentication is key!

Biblically–Based Expectations

The approach used in this article to conceptualize the nature of discipleship equipping is to identify the major biblically–based expectations incumbent upon all believers. Overall, it seems reasonable that all such mandates invariably fit under the epitome expectation "Be Holy." This mandate, found in both the Old (Lev 19:2) and New Testament (1 Pet 1:15), relates to being in right relationship with God and demonstrating the "fruit" of that relationship. More specifically, in both the Old and New Testaments, to be Holy meant to be set apart, unique, and distinct from the non-believers life-style. To be Holy connotes imitating and being in service to God. In the Old Testament, "Holiness is to effect every area of Israelite life" (RSV footnote to Lev 18:1:22-33). The New Testament reflects the heart orientation of Jesus by enriching that term "holy" to include moral, not just ritual, significance. "Its fundamental ideas are separation, consecration, devotion to God and sharing in God's purity and abstaining from earth's defilement" (Zodhiates, 1992; 1 Pet 1:15, Strong's NT #40). Clearly, holiness addresses both inner qualities and outward behaviors. Equally clear, the concept of holiness is the highest label for comprehensively incorporating all other discipleship qualities. Christ died to present us holy to the Father (Col 1:22).

Be Holy & Other Biblical Mandates

Subsumed under that Be Holy superordinate category are the following additional mandates: Dominion Mandate, populate the earth, self-governance, love God, love self, love your neighbor, and the Great Commission. Each mandate is then subdivided into subsections of discipleship that can be specifically and intentionally addressed in the Christian education setting.

Here is a list of some of Dr. Cox's publications on Kingdom Education you would find interesting and helpful in your journey.

Cox, W. F., Jr., & Peck, R. A. (2018). Christian education as discipleship formation. *Christian Education Journal, 15*(2), 245-261.

Cox, W. F., Jr. (2015). Kingdom education. In G.T. Kurian & M. A.

Lamport (Eds.), *Encyclopedia of Christian Education* (Vol 2), Lanham, MD: Rowman & Littlefield.

Cox, W. F., Jr. (2011). Kingdom education. *Journal of Research on Christian Education, 20*(3), 330-341.

Cox, W. F., Jr., Barnum, K., & Hameloth, N. J. (2010, February/March). A nine-point lesson plan format for Christian education. *Journal of Adventist Education, 22,* 4-9.

Cox, W. F., Jr., Hameloth, N. J., & Talbot, D. P. (2007). Biblical fidelity of Christian school textbooks. *Journal of Research on Christian Education, 16,* 181-210. Retrieved from www.regent.edu/education/pdfs/publications/cox/textbooks.pdf

Cox, W. F., Jr., Barnum, K. T., & Hameloth, N. J. (2007). Lesson plan format for Christian education. *Journal of Christian Education, 50*(1). Retrieved from www.regent.edu/education/pdfs/publications/cox/lesson_plan.pdf

Cox, W. F., Jr. (2001). Transforming school culture to expressions of worship and fellowship: Transformation, not just performance. In Association of Christian Schools International (Ed.), *Leadership Academy report* (pp. 34-40). Colorado Springs, CO: Association of Christian Schools International. Retrieved from www.regent.edu/education/pdfs/publications/cox/Expressions_ Worship_ Fellowship.pdf

Cox, W. F., Jr., Arroyo, A. A., & Bostain, D. (1999). Developing a nurturance teaching model. In D. C. Elliott & S. D. Holtrop (Eds.), *Nurturing and reflective teachers: A Christian approach for the 21st century* (pp. 129-140). Claremont, CA: Learning Light Educational Consulting and Publishing. Retrieved from www.regent.edu/education/pdfs/publications/cox/nurturance_ teaching_ model.pdf

The following documents are used courtesy of the Foundation for American Christian Education, the home of the Principle Approach®. These and many other free resources are available at FACE.net.

Principle Approach Education

Seven Leading Ideas of America's Christian History and Government

by Rosalie June Slater

Reprinted from *Teaching and Learning: The Principle Approach®*

1. THE CHRISTIAN IDEA OF MAN AND GOVERNMENT

The Christian History of the Constitution of the United States of America (CHOC I), pp. 1–2. See also, *Teaching and Learning: The Principle Approach* (T&L), pp. 306–310.

When our Lord, Jesus Christ, appeared among men, women and children, He honored each individual with *the Christian idea of man*. The Christian Idea Of Man, CHOC I, page 2, states:

> Christianity then appeared with its central doctrine, that man was created in the Divine image, and destined for immortality; pronouncing, that, in the eyes of God, all men are equal. This asserted for the individual an independent value. It occasioned the great inference, that man is superior to the State, which ought to be fashioned for his use. This was the advent of a new spirit and a new power in the world.

However it took centuries until there was a form of government established which would honor the individual and make the individual the "fountain of power" in the nation. The chart on page 270C of CHOC I, indicates how man, governed by God through His Word, is the source of government in America. Here, too, we find the standard of character for our representatives at all levels of government.

Read For Yourself: The Palfrey quote under the chart on page 270C of Christian History, gives us a standard of American Christian character.

2. THE CHAIN OF CHRISTIANITY MOVES WESTWARD

CHOC I, pp. 4–9. See also T&L, pp. 311–316.

Arnold Guyot, Christian Geographer, who taught at Princeton, in the 1850s, identified the northern continents as "the Continents of History." These continents trace the Westward course of the Gospel

with the Christian Idea of Man, as it found soil favorable to its development. Guyot discovered that each continent had *an individuality which God had formed to fit it for the purpose of His Story.*

Read For Yourself: CHOC I, pp. 3–5

Asia: the continent of origins (Genesis 2:8)
Europe: the continent of development (Acts 16:9–15)
America: to become the continent of "the most complete expression of Christian civilization." (Psalm 72:8)

The Map on page 6A of CHOC I, follows the path of liberty with those "signs following" to which our Lord referred. From the time of Moses and the Law, to Jesus Christ and the Gospel of Grace, the Christian idea of man flowed westward, seeking a land where each individual might be protected in their God-given life, liberty, productivity. This was God's purpose in establishing America and allowing Biblical principles of self- and civil government to flower in the establishment of our Constitutional Republic.

Read For Yourself: CHOC I, page 8, middle paragraph, where we see how God sent men and women from every continent to America to bring "the common contributions of character, energy and activity to the support and enlargement of a common country, and the spread of its influence and enlightenment through all the lands of their origin."

Read in T&L, last paragraph, page 43 and page 44, how each race and each nation have contributed to America.

3. THE PRINCIPLE OF REPRESENTATION

CHOC I, pp. 10–16. See also, T&L, pp. 317–323.

Connecticut's Founder, Reverend Thomas Hooker, preached a sermon on market day, May 31, 1638. Reverend Hooker identified God's Biblical principle of representation and his sermon known as the "Fundamental Orders of Connecticut" became the basis of our first Colonial Constitution.

Read For Yourself: CHOC I, pp. 248–257. The Connecticut Republic was an early model for the Constitution of the United States of America.

4. THE REPUBLICANISM OF CHRISTIANITY

CHOC I, pp. 16–28. See also, T&L, pp. 314–331.

The churches of primitive Christianity were "little republics." They were local institutions, each responsible to Christ. But lack of vigilance allowed centralization to gain a foothold, and many centuries passed before the English Pilgrims sought to recover the Primitive Gospel and throw off anti-Christian bondage.

Christian Principles Produce Local Self-Government. Every religion represents a form of government. "Christianity in its essence, its doctrines, and its forms is republican."

5. THE BIBLE IN ENGLISH

CHOC I, pp. 28A–36. See also, T&L, pp. 332–342.

For centuries God's Word was locked up in scholarly languages. In order for the individual man or woman to learn God's Principles of liberty, it was necessary to be able to have the Word available in a language they could learn how to read. In England, John Wyclif, the "morning star of the Reformation," translated the Bible into English. For 200 years the English Bible became a textbook of liberty—and our English Heritage of law, language, and literature, was an outgrowth of Englishmen becoming "the people of the Book."

In the early 1600s the English Colonists brought the Bible to America where it became our educational and political textbook of God's principles of liberty. God had reserved America for a Bible-reasoning, Bible-writing people who would educate their children and write their documents of government according to Gods Word.

6. CHRISTIAN RIGHTS AND ENGLISH LAW

CHOC I, pp. 37–50. See also, T&L, pp. 343–352.

Our Lord taught us "Ye shall know the truth, and the truth shall make you free." Liberty begins internally, but it must have its external expression. Freedom from sin—salvation—also includes governmental liberty. Christianity brings self and civil liberty. Because the Bible had always influenced England, even before it appeared in the language of the people, the Christian idea of man was evident in the early days of Anglo-Saxon and Anglo-Norman England. So, it is not surprising that England's most important piece of paper, the Magna Charta, or Great Charter, the first governmental expression of the rights of Englishmen, appeared in 1215 a.d. It would take centuries before this declaration became the basis of our American Bill of Rights.

Religion played a role in government, too. But the Puritan Politics of the seventeenth century was unsuccessful in endeavoring to "regulate" the behavior of men by law. The Pilgrim took reformation upon himself and separated from the state church to form the independent self-governing church, in England, in Holland, and finally in America.

7. **PRINCIPLES OF CHRISTIANITY AND GOVERNMENT**

CHOC I, pp. 372–390; 50A–125. See also T&L, pp. 353–362, "A Biblical-Political Index to John Locke."

CHOC I, pages 372–390, show how America connected "the principles of civil government with the principles of Christianity." The Bible became "the great political textbook of the patriots," page 375.

American Christians were a reading-reasoning-writing people. They studied the philosophers of liberty—researched Biblically the principles of liberty. John Locke was called the Philosopher of the American Revolution. Our American pastors loved to study his writings on life, liberty and the protection of individual property and productivity.

In the "Biblical-Political Index to John Locke" you will see how we came to some of our most important ideals for American government, and you will discover their Biblical source:

"A state of liberty is not a state of licence." Virtue is a condition of liberty.

"Man is God's Property."

"Conscience is the most sacred of all property."

"By consent were all men equal, till by that same consent, men set rulers over themselves. So that political societies all began by voluntary union."

"The great and chief end and purpose of men uniting themselves into Commonwealths, and putting themselves under government, is the preservation of their property."

LEARNING TO REASON WITH THE BIBLICAL PRINCIPLES OF GOVERNMENT

These Seven Biblical Principles first identified the Biblical Principles which were the foundation of our American Christian Constitutional Republic. They are also the Biblical principles by which God governs the individual to produce the Christian character which will support a Republic. These principles can be taught to the youngest child. Defined Biblically and historically in T&L, they key into the documentary CHOC I. This material is found in the "key" to each Principle.

The Seven Principles of America's Christian History from which we reason governmentally, are found on pages 63 and 111 of T&L. The first principle—God's Principle of Individuality—is written large, for from it flow all the other principles. This is in essence the Christian Idea of Man being identified in the life and government of the individual. It is the goal which God has for all nations.

THE FOUNDATION FOR AMERICAN CHRISTIAN EDUCATION 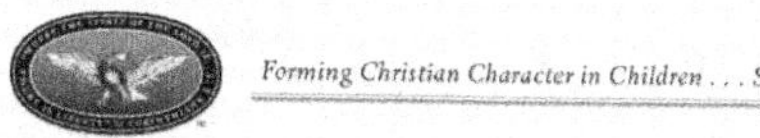 *Forming Christian Character in Children . . . Since 1965!*

I. GOD'S PRINCIPLE OF INDIVIDUALITY

T&L, pp. 65–68 and 113–117
KEY: pp. 141–183

We state this principle Biblically and then follow it historically. On page 154 of the KEY we find how this principle is illustrated in God's Word and the individuality of the writers He chose to bring His message to mankind. On page 155 we teach each individual the verse, Starting With Me:

God made me special –
Like no one else you see.
God made me a witness
To His diversity.

What follows are points which illustrate the distinctions which God gives each individual He creates.

T&L, pages 156–183 provide an overview of the historical appearing of God's Principle of Individuality. It begins with the remarkable work of Arnold Guyot, Christian Geographer, who identified the Continents which God created for His Story to be Geographic Individuals. What a wonderful way to glorify our Creator as we teach geography from His Story of men and nations!

II. THE CHRISTIAN PRINCIPLE OF SELF-GOVERNMENT

T&L, pp. 69–72 and 119–121 give the Biblical statement of the Principle and its Overview in CHOC I
KEY: pp. 184–209

Here you will find teaching information as this principle appears in America's CHOC I. On page 188 are two charts which begin to describe the action of a self-governing student at home or in school.

On page 189 we find those Pilgrim qualities of self-government which became to important to our nation:

Thrift – Economy
Industry & Initiative
Self-Reliance & Confidence

As we survey our Colonial History we can see how important Christian self-government became as God gave us 150 years of preparation in all the Colonies to become *one nation under God*, able to be self-governing.

III. AMERICA'S HERITAGE OF CHRISTIAN CHARACTER

T&L, pp. 73–75 and 123–124

KEY: pp. 210–224

The Pilgrims of England who came to America, looked to the first century Christians for their model of character. From these early Christians they learned to practice the following qualities:

Faith & Steadfastness
Brotherly Love & Christian Care
Diligence & Industry
Liberty of Conscience

William Bradford wrote our first American Christian Classic in his account of the Pilgrims. Since he was a teenager himself and took part in so many of the Pilgrim adventures, his book is a moving Christian testimony to that character which became a model for our nation. You can read an excerpt from History *Of Plimoth Plantation* in CHOC I, beginning on page 182, with a contrast between Pilgrims and Puritans.

IV. "CONSCIENCE IS THE MOST SACRED OF ALL PROPERTY"

T&L, pp. 77–78 and 125–127

KEY: pp. 225–239

This statement by James Madison, Father of our Constitution, reflects our Biblical conviction that "we are the Workmanship" of God. We must have a "conscience void of offence" to God and man. And, as John Locke wrote, "consent is our title to conscience."

We can teach this principle to our youngest child in these words, found on page 230 of the *KEY* to this principle of Property:

I am God's Property
God made me for His Purpose
He fashioned me to be
An image for His glory,
Almighty Father He.

Our property is represented in our God-given talents and our use of them for the service of the Lord. We are also given the responsibility of stewardship—the care of all that God created. Property needs to be protected and preserved, and that is the "end and purpose of government." Only a Christian Constitutional Republic can properly preserve our rights of conscience as well as the external property which we have produced.

In our American History a turning point came when our Colonists took a firm stand for No TAXATION WITHOUT REPRESENTATION.

V. THE CHRISTIAN FORM OF OUR GOVERNMENT

T&L, pp. 79–81 and 129–130

KEY: pp. 240–249

Both the Law and the Gospel are foundational to America's Christian Constitutional form of government. Our Founding Generations looked to Deuteronomy 1:13, 15 for the principle of representation:

> Take you wise men, and understanding and known among your tribes, and I will make them rulers over you . . . captains over thousands, and captains over hundreds, and captains over fifties, and captains over tens, and officers among your tribes.

READ FOR YOURSELF in CHOC I, pages 248–251, how Pastor Thomas Hooker preached a sermon on these verses and this produced America's first Constitution, known as the Fundamental Orders of Connecticut.

The Separation of Powers, or the Legislative, Executive, and Judicial aspect of our governmental action, is found in Isaiah 33:22, "For the Lord is our judge, the Lord is our lawgiver, the Lord is our king . . ."

How do we teach these principles of government to our youngest children? Government begins with individual action. When the individual child or adult Christian plans some action—perhaps it is as simple as coming home from school or taking a vacation—he or she is in effect legislating.

Putting a plan into action is the executive function. And when we review our action, from both our internal conscience, or from the external law of the land, we are performing a judicial function. (T&L, p. 244)

Determining what area of government is the supreme law of the land, we consider the State and the Nation which operate over the same territory. If we consider the two commandments of our Lord, we shall recognize that the supreme law of the land is the nation first, then the state. Thus when we travel outside our country, we are not protected as citizens because we are Virginians, Californians, Arizonians, but because we are Americans.

The Pastors of America preached in churches, in the halls of government in their election sermons, for the artillery companies, on fast days and days of Thanksgiving. They taught Biblical principles of self- and civil government. Oh that we had such pastoral leadership today to clearly identify the force and power of government to be Christ in the life of the individual American.

VI. HOW THE SEED OF LOCAL SELF-GOVERNMENT IS PLANTED

T&L, pp. 83–84 and 131–133

KEY: pp. 250–261

America's Samuel was Samuel Adams of Boston, who gave an example of uniting the American Colonies "not by external bonds, but by the vital force of distinctive ideas and principles." (T&L, p. 257) His Committees of Correspondence prepared the Colonies to clearly understand Biblical principles of government so that they could take the proper action when these principles were threatened.

Samuel Adams taught the principles of Liberty under Law, once again beginning in the Christian character of each American. He wrote:

> While the People are virtuous they cannot be subdued; but when once they lose their Virtue they will be ready to surrender their Liberties to the first external or internal Invader . . . If Virtue and Knowledge are diffused among the People, they will never be enslaved. This will be their great Security. (T&L, p. 251)

VII. THE CHRISTIAN PRINCIPLE OF AMERICAN POLITICAL UNION

T&L, pp. 85–87 and 135–136

KEY: pp. 262–268

Consistent with the Biblical principle that purpose and action begin within, our nation came together internally, two years before we declared our Independence as a separate nation under God. The occasion was the punitive action which England took against Boston, because the tea was dumped into the harbor in December of 1773—the well-known Boston Tea Party.

England discounted the Biblical education of our American Colonies. She expected that when she closed the Port of Boston on June 3, 1774, that the other colonies would take advantage of Boston's economic distress and grasp her trade. But instead, they began with a Day of Fasting and Prayer throughout the colonies. After that each of the other colonies sent aid to Boston. They gave not only prayer support, but sent food and other assistance, so that Boston could endure her economic blockade. The outpouring of loving help emphasized the internal unity. Externally, each colony appointed delegates to a First Continental Congress so that they might together determine their united action.

AMERICAN UNITY IS CHRISTIAN UNITY.

Using the Impact to History Charts

Charts are given on pp. 17–19 for use as tools for the study of providential history. Below, each chart is explained with directions for its use in studying "People Who Impacted History," "Events Which Impacted History," and "Writings Which Impacted History."

In the Pilgrim story, the following people, events, and writings should be charted for a thorough study:

People: William Bradford; John Robinson; Elder Brewster

Events: Bradford assigns private property; Thanksgiving 1623; the drought

Writings: The Mayflower Compact

PEOPLE WHO IMPACTED HISTORY

Purpose: The Key Individual Chart is a tool for ordering and recording one's research and study of biography to identify the Hand of God in the life of an individual and that individual's response (cause to effect). The individual's physical, intellectual, spiritual, and emotional characteristics, as well as his tastes, affections, and personality are charted noting how he governed and disposed his temperament, how he was steward of his internal and external property, and how he contributed to God's Gospel purpose.

Method: Statements or quotes are recorded which identify and describe each area of significance. Citations to documents and page numbers should be noted as well.

Directions:

Providential Setting: The settings, both of time and place, in which God placed this person throughout the individual's life on earth, are recorded here.

Spheres of Influence: The influences God used to develop and refine this person's internal character as well as his skills, abilities, knowledge, and talents are noted. In addition, the spheres of influence that God gave this person to impact can be noted.

Character: The attributes of the person's external traits and internal character virtues or vices which are marked or prominent, are recorded in this column.

Contributions: Note the contribution(s) the person made to forward or hinder the Gospel and liberty for individuals and nations — the Chain of Christianity® moving westward, and/or to promote the advancement of the understanding of the subject.

EVENTS WHICH IMPACTED HISTORY

Purpose: The Key Event Chart is a tool for ordering and recording one's research and study of an historical event or natural phenomenon to identify the Hand of God in advancing His kingdom (God's government and Gospel purpose, and His advancement of liberty for individuals and nations) even though there might appear to be hindrances to the same.

Method: Statements or quotes from source materials and documents are recorded which identify and describe each area of significance. Citations to documents and page numbers should be noted as well.

Directions:

Causes: What were the internal causes of the event? What was the sequence of external occurrences that led to the event?

Individuals: Which individuals and nations were involved? Was their involvement by active or tacit consent?

Actions: What were the choices and actions of the individuals and nations involved? What were the internal causes (beliefs, worldview, convictions) of the individuals and representatives of nations that produced their choices and actions?

Effects: What effects or consequences were produced by the event on life, the Gospel purpose, liberty, the revelation and understanding of the subject?

WRITINGS WHICH IMPACTED HISTORY

Purpose: The Key Document Chart is a tool for ordering and recording one's research and study of various writings, speeches, literary works, theses, or other documents of significance to discern the leading ideas and principles of any Subject—or a Key Individual's (or Nation's) worldview and presuppositions.

Method: Statements or quotes from source materials and documents are recorded which identify and describe each area of significance. Citations to documents and page numbers should be noted as well.

Directions:

Principles: Causative Truths and Presuppositions

Leading Ideas: Axioms, Catechisms, Definitions, Established Principles and Properties of the Subject, Ideals, Questions, Quotes, Prompts, Statements of Fact, Themes, Topics—any way that ideas of consequence are clothed with words.

Specific Quotes: "Quotations from the document" or paraphrases of significant excerpts (with explanations of the reasoning and relating of the quote to the principle or leading idea included).

PEOPLE WHO IMPACTED HISTORY: ____________

Providential Setting	Spheres of Influence	Character	Contributions

May Be Duplicated

WRITINGS WHICH IMPACTED HISTORY: ______

Principles & Leading Ideas	Specific Quotes

May Be Duplicated

EVENTS WHICH IMPACTED HISTORY: ____________

Causes	Individuals	Actions	Effects

PEOPLE WHO IMPACTED HISTORY: Noah Webster – Father of American Education & Scholarship

God's Providence

1. Webster's Family Heritage:
   A. **Father** – Noah, Sr. – descended from Puritan named John Webster (came to American in 1630s and followed Thomas Hooker to CT) who became governor of CT; he was rugged, Yankee farmer, served in French & Indian War; as a deacon in a Congregational Church, and as Justice of the Peace in West Hartford; intelligent & wise; his counsel was often sought in the community.
   B. **Mother** – Mercy Steele – great granddaughter of Gov. William Bradford of Plymouth Plantation; she was of great intelligence, gentle & loving in all her ways.
   C. Noah was fourth of five children who all lived long, productive lives.
      Born: October 16, 1758 on an 80-acre farm in West Hartford, CT
   D. Married *Rebecca Greenleaf*: witty, sensible, gay, & social woman at age of 30.
   E. Had seven living children (6 daughters and 1 son) whom he educated and continued a correspondence with all through life.
   F. He had many grandchildren, whom he loved.

2. Providentially in Philadelphia during Constitutional Convention; his wisdom was sought often by the delegates.

3. Converted at age of 49 and made a public confession in church in 1808 just prior to beginning his work on the *Dictionary*.

Webster's Credo of Education – ***Laying cornerstone at Amherst college, 1820***

"The object of this institution . . . is one of the noblest which can occupy the attention and claim the contributions of the Christian republic. It is to second the efforts of the apostles themselves, in extending and establishing the Redeemer's empire – the empire of truth. It is to aid in the important work of raising the human race from ignorance and debasement; to enlighten their minds; to exalt their character; and to teach them the way to happiness and to glory. Too long have men been engaged in the barbarous works of multiplying the miseries of human life. Too long have their exertions and resources been devoted to war and plunder; to the destruction of lives and property; to the ravage of cities; to the unnatural, the monstrous employment of enslaving and degrading their own species. Blessed be our lot! We live to see a new era in the history of man – an era when reason and religion begin to resume their sway, and to impress the heavenly truth, that the appropriate business of men, is to imitate the Savior; to serve their God; and bless their fellow men."

Spheres of Influence

1. **Home, Family & Farm life in Connecticut:**
   Lonely for children and provided long hours of work
   Noah expected to perform many tasks on the farm for his father who early trained him to severe and unremitting industry: early rising, strict temperance, vigorous exercise which all prolonged Noah's life
   Connecticut enjoyed more self-government than any other colony and its Constitution was a model for the U.S. Constitution;
   West Hartford – thrifty, industrious farming town
   Three influences in Connecticut that shaped thinking:
   a. Yankee philosophy of hard work
   b. Town Meeting form of civil government
   c. Congregational Church (State church) – Calvinism
   Blessing from his parents upon leaving for Yale:
   "We wish to have you serve your generation and do good in the world and be useful and may you so behave as to gain the esteem of all virtuous people that are acquainted with you; and gain a comfortable subsistence, but especially that you may so live as to obtain the favor of Almighty God and His grace in this world and a saving interest in the merits of Jesus Christ, without which no man can be happy."

2. **Church:** His family attended the Congregational Church; active in music; father – deacon; as an adult he served in the church

3. **Education and Schooling:**
   Connecticut had state law requiring elementary education 11 mo./yr.
   Noah attended when he wasn't needed on the farm
   Books: Psalter, KJV Bible, N.E. Primer; Christian Catechism
   Tutored for college entrance by Rev. Nathan Perkins for 2 years
   Entered Yale College at age of 15. Met G. Washington on campus.
   1778 – Graduated with B.A.
   Read Law with Olliver Ellsworth
   1781 – Admitted to the Bar
   1781 – received his M.A. Degree from Yale for his dissertation
   1822 – received LL.D. from Yale

4. **Friends and Associates** – were all men of powerful intellect:
   Noah's Yale Graduating Class – Most Distinguished class until the Civil War: Joel Barlow – Poet; Alexander Wolcott & Abraham Bishop – Jefferson Compatriots; Zephaniah Swift – CT's greatest jurist; John Trumbull; Oliver Wolcott – Secretary of the Treasury; Uriah Tracy – U.S. Senator; Josiah Meigs – President of U. of Georgia
   Other Friends: George Washington; John Adams; John Jay; Timothy Puckering; Benjamin Franklin; James Madison, Benjamin Rush; Alexander Hamilton

5. **Noah's Hero:** "the great genius – the immortal Newton"

Christian History Chart, The Noah Plan © 1997 Foundation for American Christian Education

PEOPLE WHO IMPACTED HISTORY: Noah Webster – Father of American Education & Scholarship – page 2

Character

1. **Physical Appearance:**
   Tall and erect
   Slender, lithe, Yankee form
   Auburn hair; gray-blue eyes, square jaw
   Ruddy complexion
   Excellent health (but complained of ill health all his life)

2. **Internal Character:**
   Lively disposition
   Sanguine temperament (warm, ardent, and confident)
   Energetic and enterprising
   Lover and defender of truth
   Honest
   Frank in his speech
   Generous with his time, counsel, and pen
   Thrifty with resources
   Bold, original thinker; candid mind
   Witty quick memory
   Eager love for learning, loved books
   Self-confident as a leader
   Polite – had a refinement of thought and feelings
   Thorough and precise
   Hard-working, diligent
   Self-reliant and persevering
   Patriotic and passionately interested in the welfare of our country
   Had no pride of opinion – was willing to change if incorrect
   Was *The Prompter* – sat behind the scenes to correct error and assist the memory

3. **Life Time Habits:**
   Studied the Bible daily and prayed every morning after rising
   Maintained a daily schedule for writing, reading, and other tasks
   Set aside time each day to be with his family
   Maintained various jobs at the same time
   Performed original investigation and research
   Arranged all his acquired knowledge in a most exact order
   Kept a daily journal
   Preserved documents carefully, filed articles he read and wrote
   Marked all new words, corrected errors in margins of his books, kept references to corresponding passages in other works
   His method was his presiding principle of life
   His son-in-law, Chauncey Goodrich, said these qualities sustained Noah through difficulties that would have crushed other men's spirits.

4. **Quotes:**
   "Education is useless without the Bible."
   "An immense effect may be produced by small powers wisely and steadily directed."
   "The basis of all excellence in writing and conversation is truth – truth is intellectual gold, which is as durable as it is splendid and valuable."
   "In my view, the Christian religion is the most important and one of the first things in which all children ought to be instructed."
   "All government originates in families, and if neglected there, it will hardly exist in society . . . the foundation of all free government and social order must be laid in families and in the discipline of youth."

Contributions

1. **Educator – America's Greatest Schoolmaster:**
   Educated his own children
   Taught school while he studied law
   First teacher to develop a civics course
   Head, Episcopal School in Philadelphia
   Simplified spelling providing principles and pronunciation
   Taught millions of Americans to read
   Taught music

2. **Founder & President of Amherst College**

3. **Lexicographer:** Recognized the American language was different than England's language and wrote first American Dictionary
   Master of over 26 languages
   Made a profound study of philology and etymology of words
   Included over 70,000 words
   Took him nearly 20 years to complete (70 years old)
   Wrote Biblical definitions & exhortations
   Contained scientific terms – was more like an encyclopedia
   Changed and unified spelling
   Included 20,000 new words
   Reflected America's Christian philosophy of life & government

4. **Lawyer & Judge:**
   Fought for and secured copyright laws in America
   Fought for uniform patent laws
   Active in anti-slavery movement
   Served as Judge in state court system
   Boston General Court member
   Representative from New Haven in State legislature

5. **Defender of the U.S. Constitution:**
   Wrote "Sketches of American Policy"
   Proposed and fought for a U.S. Constitution
   Traveled around the new nation to promote the ratification

6. **Author, Editor, & Publisher:** Wrote on a greater variety of topics than any other U.S. author
   Text books:
   "Blue-Backed Speller" – backbone of American Education (revealed the spirit of liberty and independence for it used a self-taught method); over 100 million published by 1910 – more than any other book in America)
   Readers – one contained geography & history of the United States
   Grammar Book
   Histories
   Catechism for U.S. Constitution
   Introduced Biology to Children
   Began a literary magazine (*American Magazine*) and *The Prompter*
   He translated the Bible

7. **Natural Scientist**
   He compiled and wrote a *History of Epidemic Disease* which Johns Hopkins still uses today

Bibliography

American Dictionary of the English Language (1828) by Noah Webster – added biography, "Noah Webster: Founding Father of American Education" by Rosalie J. Slater, F.A.C.E. 1967.

The Life and Testimony of Noah Webster, by Chauncey A. Goodrich, quoted in *Teaching and Learning America's Christian History*, Appendix, pp. 280–301.

Noah Webster: Schoolmaster to America, by Harry R. Warfel, Macmillan Co., NY, 1936.

Christian History Chart, The Noah Plan © 1997 Foundation for American Christian Education

KINGDOM OF HEAVEN SCRIPTURES

Matthew 3:2

…and saying, "Repent, for the kingdom of heaven has come near."

Matthew 4:17

From that time on Jesus began to preach, "Repent, for the kingdom of heaven has come near."

Matthew 5:3

"Blessed are the poor in spirit, for theirs is the kingdom of heaven."

Matthew 5:10

"Blessed are those who are persecuted because of righteousness, for theirs is the kingdom of heaven."

Matthew 5:19

"Therefore anyone who sets aside one of the least of these commands and teaches others accordingly will be called least in the kingdom of heaven, but whoever practices and teaches these commands will be called great in the kingdom of heaven."

Matthew 5:20

"For I tell you that unless your righteousness surpasses that of the Pharisees and the teachers of the law, you will certainly not enter the kingdom of heaven."

Matthew 7:21

[True and False Disciples] "Not everyone who says to me, 'Lord, Lord,' will enter the kingdom of heaven, but only the one who does the will of my Father who is in heaven."

Matthew 8:11

"I say to you that many will come from the east and the west, and will take their places at the feast with Abraham, Isaac and Jacob in the kingdom of heaven."

Matthew 10:7

"As you go, proclaim this message: 'The kingdom of heaven has come near.'"

Matthew 11:11

"Truly I tell you, among those born of women there has not risen anyone greater than John the Baptist; yet whoever is least in the kingdom of heaven is greater than he."

Matthew 11:12

"From the days of John the Baptist until now, the kingdom of heaven has been subjected to violence, and violent people have been raiding it."

Matthew 13:11

He replied, "Because the knowledge of the secrets of the kingdom of heaven has been given to you, but not to them."

Matthew 13:24

[The Parable of the Weeds] "Jesus told them another parable: 'The kingdom of heaven is like a man who sowed good seed in his field.'"

Matthew 13:31

[The Parables of the Mustard Seed and the Yeast] "He told them another parable: 'The kingdom of heaven is like a mustard seed, which a man took and planted in his field.'"

Matthew 13:33

"He told them still another parable: 'The kingdom of heaven is like yeast that a woman took and mixed into about sixty pounds of flour until it worked all through the dough.'"

Matthew 13:44

[The Parables of the Hidden Treasure and the Pearl] "The kingdom of heaven is like treasure hidden in a field. When a man found it, he hid it again, and then in his joy went and sold all he had and bought that field."

Matthew 13:45

"Again, the kingdom of heaven is like a merchant looking for fine pearls."

Matthew 13:47

[The Parable of the Net] "Once again, the kingdom of heaven is like a net that was let down into the lake and caught all kinds of fish."

Matthew 13:52

He said to them, "Therefore every teacher of the law who has become a disciple in the kingdom of heaven is like the owner of a house who brings out of his storeroom new treasures as well as old."

Matthew 16:19

"I will give you the keys of the kingdom of heaven; whatever you bind on earth will be bound in heaven, and whatever you loose on earth will be loosed in heaven."

Matthew 18:1

[The Greatest in the Kingdom of Heaven] "At that time the disciples came to Jesus and asked, 'Who, then, is the greatest in the kingdom of heaven?'"

Matthew 18:3

"And he said: 'Truly I tell you, unless you change and become like little children, you will never enter the kingdom of heaven.'"

Matthew 18:4

"Therefore, whoever takes the lowly position of this child is the greatest in the kingdom of heaven."

Matthew 18:23

"Therefore, the kingdom of heaven is like a king who wanted to settle accounts with his servants."

Matthew 19:12

"For there are eunuchs who were born that way, and there are eunuchs who have been made eunuchs by others—and there are those who choose to live like eunuchs for the sake of the kingdom of heaven. The one who can accept this should accept it."

Matthew 19:14

"Jesus said, 'Let the little children come to me, and do not hinder them, for the kingdom of heaven belongs to such as these.'"

Matthew 19:23

"Then Jesus said to his disciples, 'Truly I tell you, it is hard for someone who is rich to enter the kingdom of heaven.'"

Matthew 20:1

[The Parable of the Workers in the Vineyard] "For the kingdom of heaven is like a landowner who went out early in the morning to hire workers for his vineyard."

Matthew 22:2

"The kingdom of heaven is like a king who prepared a wedding banquet for his son."

Matthew 23:13

[Seven Woes on the Teachers of the Law and the Pharisees] "Woe to you, teachers of the law and Pharisees, you hypocrites! You shut the door of the kingdom of heaven in people's faces. You yourselves do not enter, nor will you let those enter who are trying to."

Matthew 25:1

[The Parable of the Ten Virgins] "At that time the kingdom of heaven will be like ten virgins who took their lamps and went out to meet the bridegroom."

KINGDOM OF GOD SCRIPTURES

Matthew 12:28

"But if it is by the Spirit of God that I drive out demons, then the kingdom of God has come upon you."

Matthew 19:16

[The Rich and the Kingdom of God] "Just then a man came up to Jesus and asked, 'Teacher, what good thing must I do to get eternal life?'"

Matthew 19:24

"Again I tell you, it is easier for a camel to go through the eye of a needle than for someone who is rich to enter the kingdom of God."

Matthew 21:31

"'Which of the two did what his father wanted?' 'The first,' they answered. Jesus said to them, 'Truly I tell you, the tax collectors and the prostitutes are entering the kingdom of God ahead of you.'"

Matthew 21:43

"Therefore I tell you that the kingdom of God will be taken away from you and given to a people who will produce its fruit."

Mark 1:15

"'The time has come,' he said. 'The kingdom of God has come near. Repent and believe the good news!'"

Mark 4:11

"He told them, 'The secret of the kingdom of God has been given to you. But to those on the outside everything is said in parables.'"

Mark 4:26

[The Parable of the Growing Seed] He also said, "This is what the kingdom of God is like. A man scatters seed on the ground."

Mark 4:30

[The Parable of the Mustard Seed] "Again he said, 'What shall we say the kingdom of God is like, or what parable shall we use to describe it?'"

Mark 9:1

"And he said to them, 'Truly I tell you, some who are standing here will not taste death before they see that the kingdom of God has come with power.'"

Mark 9:47

"And if your eye causes you to stumble, pluck it out. It is better for you to enter the kingdom of God with one eye than to have two eyes and be thrown into hell."

Mark 10:14

"When Jesus saw this, he was indignant. He said to them, 'Let the little children come to me, and do not hinder them, for the kingdom of God belongs to such as these.'"

Mark 10:15

"Truly I tell you, anyone who will not receive the kingdom of God like a little child will never enter it."

Mark 10:17

[The Rich and the Kingdom of God] "As Jesus started on his way, a man ran up to him and fell on his knees before him. 'Good teacher,' he asked, 'what must I do to inherit eternal life?'"

Mark 10:23

"Jesus looked around and said to his disciples, 'How hard it is for the rich to enter the kingdom of God!'"

Mark 10:24

"The disciples were amazed at his words. But Jesus said again, 'Children, how hard it is to enter the kingdom of God!'"

Mark 10:25

"It is easier for a camel to go through the eye of a needle than for someone who is rich to enter the kingdom of God."

Mark 12:34

"When Jesus saw that he had answered wisely, he said to him, 'You are not far from the kingdom of God.' And from then on no one dared ask him any more questions."

Mark 14:25

"Truly I tell you, I will not drink again from the fruit of the vine until that day when I drink it new in the kingdom of God."

Mark 15:43

"Joseph of Arimathea, a prominent member of the Council, who was himself waiting for the kingdom of God, went boldly to Pilate and asked for Jesus' body."

Luke 4:43

"But he said, 'I must proclaim the good news of the kingdom of God to the other towns also, because that is why I was sent.'"

Luke 6:20

"Looking at his disciples, he said: 'Blessed are you who are poor, for yours is the kingdom of God.'"

Luke 7:28

"I tell you, among those born of women there is no one greater than John; yet the one who is least in the kingdom of God is greater than he."

Luke 8:1

[The Parable of the Sower] "After this, Jesus traveled about from one town and village to another, proclaiming the good news of the kingdom of God. The Twelve were with him"

Luke 8:10

"He said, 'The knowledge of the secrets of the kingdom of God has been given to you, but to others I speak in parables, so that, 'though seeing, they may not see; though hearing, they may not understand.'"

Luke 9:2

"...and he sent them out to proclaim the kingdom of God and to heal the sick."

Luke 9:11

"...but the crowds learned about it and followed him. He welcomed them and spoke to them about the kingdom of God, and healed those who needed healing."

Luke 9:27

"Truly I tell you, some who are standing here will not taste death before they see the kingdom of God."

Luke 9:60

"Jesus said to him, 'Let the dead bury their own dead, but you go and proclaim the kingdom of God.'"

Luke 9:62

"Jesus replied, 'No one who puts a hand to the plow and looks back is fit for service in the kingdom of God.'"

Luke 10:9

"Heal the sick who are there and tell them, 'The kingdom of God has come near to you.'"

Luke 10:11

"Even the dust of your town we wipe from our feet as a warning to you. Yet be sure of this: The kingdom of God has come near."

Luke 11:20

"But if I drive out demons by the finger of God, then the kingdom of God has come upon you."

Luke 13:18

[The Parables of the Mustard Seed and the Yeast] "Then Jesus asked, 'What is the kingdom of Godlike? What shall I compare it to?'"

Luke 13:20

"Again he asked, 'What shall I compare the kingdom of God to?'"

Luke 13:28

"There will be weeping there, and gnashing of teeth, when you see Abraham, Isaac and Jacob and all the prophets in the kingdom of God, but you yourselves thrown out."

Luke 13:29

"People will come from east and west and north and south, and will take their places at the feast in the kingdom of God."

Luke 14:15

[The Parable of the Great Banquet] "When one of those at the table with him heard this, he said to Jesus, 'Blessed is the one who will eat at the feast in the kingdom of God.'"

Luke 16:16

[Additional Teachings] "The Law and the Prophets were proclaimed until John. Since that time, the good news of the kingdom of God is being preached, and everyone is forcing their way into it."

Luke 17:20

[The Coming of the Kingdom of God] "Once, on being asked by the Pharisees when the kingdom of God would come, Jesus replied, 'The coming of the kingdom of God is not something that can be observed.'"

Luke 17:21

"Nor will people say, 'Here it is,' or 'There it is,' because the kingdom of God is in your midst."

Luke 18:16

"But Jesus called the children to him and said, 'Let the little children come to me, and do not hinder them, for the kingdom of God belongs to such as these.'"

Luke 18:17

"Truly I tell you, anyone who will not receive the kingdom of God like a little child will never enter it."

In Context | Full Chapter | Other Translations

Luke 18:18

[The Rich and the Kingdom of God] "A certain ruler asked him, 'Good teacher, what must I do to inherit eternal life?'"

Luke 18:24

"Jesus looked at him and said, 'How hard it is for the rich to enter the kingdom of God!'"

Luke 18:25

"Indeed, it is easier for a camel to go through the eye of a needle than for someone who is rich to enter the kingdom of God."

Luke 18:29

"'Truly I tell you,' Jesus said to them, 'no one who has left home or wife or brothers or sisters or parents or children for the sake of the kingdom of God.'"

Luke 19:11

[The Parable of the Ten Minas] "While they were listening to this, he went on to tell them a parable, because he was near Jerusalem and the people thought that the kingdom of God was going to appear at once."

Luke 21:31

"Even so, when you see these things happening, you know that the kingdom of God is near."

Luke 22:16

"For I tell you, I will not eat it again until it finds fulfillment in the kingdom of God."

Luke 22:18

"For I tell you I will not drink again from the fruit of the vine until the kingdom of God comes."

Luke 23:51

"...who had not consented to their decision and action. He came from the Judean town of Arimathea, and he himself was waiting for the kingdom of God."

John 3:3

"Jesus replied, 'Very truly I tell you, no one can see the kingdom of God unless they are born again.'"

John 3:5

"Jesus answered, 'Very truly I tell you, no one can enter the kingdom of God unless they are born of water and the Spirit.'"

Acts 1:3

"After his suffering, he presented himself to them and gave many convincing proofs that he was alive. He appeared to them over a period of forty days and spoke about the kingdom of God."

Acts 8:12

"But when they believed Philip as he proclaimed the good news of the kingdom of God and the name of Jesus Christ, they were baptized, both men and women."

Acts 14:22

"...strengthening the disciples and encouraging them to remain true to the faith. 'We must go through many hardships to enter the kingdom of God,' they said."

Acts 19:8

"Paul entered the synagogue and spoke boldly there for three months, arguing persuasively about the kingdom of God."

Acts 28:23

"They arranged to meet Paul on a certain day, and came in even larger numbers to the place where he was staying. He witnessed to them from morning till evening, explaining about the kingdom of God, and from the Law of Moses and from the Prophets he tried to persuade them about Jesus."

Acts 28:31

"He proclaimed the kingdom of God and taught about the Lord Jesus Christ—with all boldness and without hindrance!"

Romans 14:17

"For the kingdom of God is not a matter of eating and drinking, but of righteousness, peace and joy in the Holy Spirit."

1 Corinthians 4:20

"For the kingdom of God is not a matter of talk but of power."

1 Corinthians 6:9

"Or do you not know that wrongdoers will not inherit the kingdom of God? Do not be deceived: Neither the sexually immoral nor idolaters nor adulterers nor men who have sex with men."

1 Corinthians 6:10

"...nor thieves nor the greedy nor drunkards nor slanderers nor swindlers will inherit the kingdom of God."

1 Corinthians 15:50

"I declare to you, brothers and sisters, that flesh and blood cannot inherit the kingdom of God, nor does the perishable inherit the imperishable."

Galatians 5:21

"...and envy; drunkenness, orgies, and the like. I warn you, as I did before, that those who live like this will not inherit the kingdom of God."

Colossians 4:11

"Jesus, who is called Justus, also sends greetings. These are the only Jews among my co-workers for the kingdom of God, and they have proved a comfort to me."

2 Thessalonians 1:5

"All this is evidence that God's judgment is right, and as a result you will be counted worthy of the kingdom of God, for which you are suffering."

THY KINGDOM COME – PRAYER PRINCIPLES

by Dr. Claudia Berry

Holy Scriptures declare that when the Kingdom of God has come to us, the life-giving message of the Christian faith is *Freedom*. Jesus spoke clearly of freedom and liberty; He prayed, *"Thy Kingdom come and* Thy will be done on earth as it is in heaven…" (Matt 6:10). There is no bondage in heaven and His purpose in coming to earth was "to preach deliverance to the captives…to set at liberty them that are bruised" (Luke 4:18; Isa 61:1).

- *"It was for freedom that Christ set us free...do not be subject again to a yoke of slavery." (Gal 5:1 NASB).*
- *"Now the Lord is the Spirit, and where the Spirit of the Lord is, there is liberty."* (2 Cor. 3:17).
- *You will know the truth and the truth will make you free."* (John 8:32).

How do we *gain this freedom* that Christ offers in such a way that we are eternally free from the slavery of sin, evil, and wickedness that is in the world all around us? And how does the Kingdom of God come into hearts and lives?

Freedom is an outcome of the sacrificial death of Jesus Christ on the cross. The plan of God was to redeem, or buy back, the human race stolen from Him when Eve and Adam bought Satan's lies and deceit in the Garden of Eden. God had initially put humanity on Earth to fellowship with Him and to have dominion over the earth. But, He had given mankind the choice to remain in fellowship or follow other voices. Eve and Adam entertained the voice of deceit and fell from God's good plan and into the slavery of Satan. *Freedom* had to come from our Creator, and its cost was the sacrifice of God's Son, Jesus, to overcome the immense hold of sin that had so permeated human nature.

PRAYER PRINCIPLE

Human choice must again be the key to obtaining *freedom*. The individual whose heart longs for freedom from the slavery of sin obtains this deliverance through

the ***prayer of confession and repentance***, the prayer that sets the captive free.

Prayer is a Principle, or a "cause" that produces the "effects" of freedom, from sin first, and subsequently into a lifetime of deliverance from its effects, both in the Believer and for people and circumstances for whom they pray. Prayer is the power of God brought down to Earth. A *principle* is defined, partially, as "In a general sense, the cause, source or origin of any thing; that from which a thing proceeds; as the principle of motion; the principles of action...Being that produces any thing; operative cause." (Webster,1828).

POWER

Power is the "faculty of moving or of producing a change in something…power of doing…power of receiving" (Webster, 1828). To exercise the power of prayer, one must stand in right relationship with Him, and the outcome must be aligned with the fundamental will of God that all mankind be saved (John 3:16, 17) and that the Kingdom of God come to earth (Luke 11:2). "Satan is said to have the *power* of death, as he introduced sin, the cause of death, temporal and eternal" (Webster, 1828). "Christ is called the *power* of God, as through Him and His gospel, God displays His *power* and authority in ransoming and saving sinners, I Cor. 1:18" (Webster, 1828).

Prayer is the power to obtain freedom from the power of sin and Satan. First by personal repentance for sin, and then asking for the blessing of the Holy Spirit unto salvation; then seeking the powerful work and drawing of God into the lives of others that bring the will and kingdom of God to earth.

The Bible is a book of the power of God to overcome death, sin, enemies, Satan, weakness, sickness, and all the problems and circumstances brought to earth by Satan. Old Testament times are filled with the power of prayer to deliver Daniel from the lion's den (Dan. 6); restore Jerusalem in Nehemiah's time (Neh. 1); to give a childless woman, Hannah, a son who would become the answer to Israel's need for leadership during corrupt times; to save Jerusalem and Judah from the cruel Assyrian King Sennacherib, leader of world's mightiest army, when King Hezekiah, King of the tiny nation of Judah, spread out his problem before the Lord (2 Kings19:14-19).

Power with God was demonstrated in the Gospels when Jesus prayed and raised Lazarus from the dead (John 11:38-44); when He prayed and fed 5,000 men, women, and children with 5 loaves of bread and two fish (Matt 14:13-21). Though Jesus had the power to do such amazing miracles, He always kept His will submitted to the Father's as when He prayed in Gethsemane to be spared the upcoming death on the cross, saying, "Father, if You willing, remove this cup from Me; *yet not My will, but Yours be done"* (Luke 22:42 NASB). It appears that the Father could trust Him with unlimited power because Jesus always kept His will submitted to the Father's and the divine Kingdom plan.

In New Testament times, Paul and Silas were freed from guards and chains in prison when an earthquake struck as they prayed and sang praises to God (Acts 16:16-40). Peter's prison chains fell from him, when an angel awakened him and led him out of prison, though he was guarded by 16 soldiers at King Herod's command, because the church was earnestly praying (Acts 12:1-18).

Throughout history, prayers of the righteous have always availed much (James 5:16). A few are noted here:

- Mary, Queen of Scots, is reputed to have said, "I fear the prayers of John Knox more than the standing armies of Europe."
- George Mueller, father of the orphanage movement in England and a man of little money, proclaimed that it was through prayer alone that he was made able to raise 10,000 orphans; he declared that he never asked human provisions, but went to God only, to obtain food, housing, clothing, and money.
- George Washington, father of America's fight for freedom, was found by a man named Isaac Potts kneeling in the snows at a critical time of the American Revolution at Valley Forge beside his horse, praying for Almighty God to intervene that the cause of liberty might prevail.

[*CLASS*: Personal stories of deliverance through prayer should be discussed to build faith, through testimony, in the power of God to deliver.]

[*NOTE*: The Principle of "power through friction," or the power of prayer aroused through desperate needs. "By rubbing (friction) you can create charges ...for generating electricity" (www.quora.-com/How-is-friction-able-to-produce-electricity). It is in the heat, or "friction" of "felt" personal needs, or the needs of others, or the anguished burden of a cause that is dear to one's heart, that the believing Christian can go to God – through the power of prayer -- and obtain help. Psalm 46:1 declares, "God is our refuge and strength, a very present help in trouble." Hebrews 4:16 invites, "Let us boldly to the throne of grace…find...help in time of need" (KJV).

Dear Christian: *"If God has invited you to bring every burden and need to Him, as He indeed has, and if others have obtained relief and blessings for their needs,* WHY NOT YOU? WHY DO YOU STILL CARRY THE LOAD THAT IS TOO HEAVY? BRING IT TO GOD THIS MOMENT AND OBTAIN THE GIFT AND THE GRACE OF *FREEDOM.*

HOW TO ENTER INTO… *PRAYER*

There are basically five general types of prayer demonstrated in the Bible: Confession, Petition, Intercession, Praise, and Thanksgiving (the Hand of Prayer); and *all* are moved by the arm of Faith. Examples:

*__*Confession*__* [pinky finger]: "If we ***confess*** our sins, He is faithful and just to forgive us our sins and to cleanse us from all unrighteousness" [I John 1:9].

*__*Petition*__* [ring finger]: "For this child I prayed, and the Lord has granted me my ***petition*** that I made to Him" [1 Samuel 1:27].

*__*Intercession*__* [tall finger]: "As for me, far be it from me that I should sin against the Lord by ceasing to ***pray for you***" [1 Samuel 12:23].

****Thanksgiving*** [pointer finger]: "Giving ***thanks*** always and for everything to God the Father in the name of our Lord Jesus Christ" [Ephesians 5:20].

****Praise*** [thumb]: "I will bless the Lord at all times; His ***praise*** shall continually be in my mouth" [Psalm 34:1].

LET US PRAY!

The power of prayer is not in the discussion of it, but in the doing, in ***praying***. *Pray that you may obtain,* is the example of Christ and the command of God.

Always...

- Pray in the Name of Jesus (Matt 18;19; 21:22; Mark 11:24; John 14:13-14; 15:7). Do not pray for something that He cannot bless.
- Lay out your "cause" before Him (2 Kings 19:14-15) as did King Hezekiah.
- Pray deeply, passionately from your heart as did King Jehoshaphat when received word of a vast military invasion of Judah (2 Chronicles 20:2-3). This chapter establishes some powerful ***prayer principles***:
- Go to God for yourself, he "set himself to seek the Lord" [v.3] rather than send for Isaiah the prophet.
- Jehoshaphat proclaimed a fast in Judah, gathered in the house of the Lord to ask *help* of the Lord [v. 4,5]. Jehoshaphat began to plead and reason with the Lord, recalling to God all His prior dealings and promises with His people, declaring the omnipotence of the Almighty and casting their existence on Him, just standing with their children, saying, "we have no might...neither do we know what to do, but our eyes are upon you" (2 Chronicles 20:12).
- The Spirit of the Lord came to Jahaziel, a Levite, after they sought the Lord giving direction and promises that still echo through the ages today to instruct praying people: "Be not afraid or dismayed...the battle is not yours but God's...You shall not need to fight in this battle...stand still and see the salvation of the Lord with you...the Lord will be with you" (vv. 15-17). The Spirit even instructed them where to go to meet their enemy!

- The king and the nation *worshipped* the Lord. Then Jehoshaphat established an enduring *principle* that still seems to warm the heart of God: He appointed singers to go out to battle ahead of the army charged with declaring, *"Praise the Lord; for his mercy endures forever"* (v. 21). When they began to sing and to praise, the Lord *ambushed* their enemies (v. 22) and the enemies destroyed each other. Judah gathered tremendous riches without having to fight the battle; God fought for them because of prayer.
- Pray without ceasing (1 Thes. 5:17).
- Pray ***against*** the powers and agents of wickedness *"Because* you have prayed *against Sennacherib* (Isaiah 37:21). God says, "I will defend this city..." and the angel of the Lord slew 185,000 Assyrian warriors sent by Sennacherib to destroy Jerusalem (vv. 35-36), and his own sons killed him and ended the 700 year old dynasty of Assyria.
- Pray to know the will of God in every situation; pray His will be done.
- Pray blessings of grace upon your family, others, your nation, leaders.... Pray **Numbers 6:22-27**, the blessing God commanded be prayed of His people.
- Upon the wicked, pray conviction and the drawing of the heart toward God.
- Ask God what act of obedience on your part will He honor that you might have the power of prayer with Him; ask Him to help you do this obedience.
- Get alone with God; Jesus often did.
- GOD *plus* ONE

The Holy Bible is a *record* of God's Word and works in His relationship with mankind. Think of how poor we would be today if God had not inspired the many authors of the various books of the Bible to *record* His Word and wonders. You too need a *record* of God's Word and works revealed and taught to you! What God has done before in lives and events can certainly be done again for He is eternal and His love and mercy are over all. *Look for the principles of cause and effect in Biblical times;* these will guide and instruct how you might ask Him to do similar things in your situation and life, while always leaving specifics to Him, but **remind Him of His inviolable Word**:

- "My Word …shall not return to me void, but it shall accomplish that which I please, and it shall prosper in the thing whereto I sent it" (Isa 55:11).
- "I will hasten My Word to perform it" (Jer 1:12).
- "Ask and you will receive…" (John 16:24).

WHEN YOU HAVE DONE ALL…WHEN NOTHING MORE CAN BE DONE AND YET THERE IS NO MANIFESTATION OF THE PROMISE…. DO NOT TAKE MATTERS IN YOUR OWN HANDS AS DID ABRAHAM AND SARAH AND HAVE AN "ISHMAEL"! A VAST MISTAKE…

INSTEAD, PRAY THE PRAYER OF RELINQUISHMENT… WAIT FOR GOD TO MAKE THE NEXT MOVE. REMEMBER… LIFE ON EARTH IS A BATTLE AND YOU ARE AIMING FOR VICTORY THROUGH THE RISEN CHRIST.

TO RECORD:

Described here is an orderly method the Holy Spirit revealed to this author to use as a *prayer notebook* that has yielded indescribable blessings and lessons. It is offered to you as a suggestion to help in your prayer journey and walk with God.

A Beginning: What is the essential time element which all humans share and by which we can measure our days? *Days of the week.* The major burdens of the heart which involve a heartfelt need to pray are associated with individuals and institutions such as nations, governments, church, and unique situations. What is the major burden of your heart *TODAY*? If today is Wednesday for example, place a tab in your notebook marked Wednesday, and pour out that burden before God for that need in your notebook.

Set up tabs for Thursday through Tuesday. Behind each tab, record the next burden and continue until each burden is recorded under a daily tab of the week. For each burden, ask God to reveal a promise for this need. It may or may not be the ultimate one that He will quicken as your Word to stand on and claim for the full conviction that He will come into that situation and redeem it. Continue to do this for every need.

Always be alert for God's Word that He is going to quicken to you, so that you know your prayers have been heard and will be answered—*in His time and in His way.*

Put a date, and even the time of day, beside every entry. You will surely find in the days, months, years ahead—and often within a day's time—something will be made evident that says God is on the scene and you will long to see a clear picture of how He is at work!

Be certain to put yourself and your journey with God under one specific daily tab. Your needs for knowledge, revelation, guidance for decisions that must be made belong here. Has God given you a Word of Promise for your life, your work, your future? Record it here just as you will record Promises for those for whom you pray.

The Promises quickened to your heart for all needs are the Word of God which He *has promised to perform.* Never let go of them, regardless how long you must wait nor how impossible the fulfillment may seem! Date everything, every entry. Pray the Promises out loud; hearing them will strengthen your belief that He is bringing to pass because "Faith comes by hearing and hearing by the Word of God" (Rom 10:17).

MANIFESTATION: *A LIFE FAITHFULLY LIVED*

Through perseverance and faith in *asking,* you will *receive* the fulfillment of God's Promise to you. Rejoice in His gift of the Promise and Praise Him before you *see* the manifestation. God honors faith in His Word and your word of *praise and thanksgiving* brings joy to the Father's heart. Continue to go deeply into the Word of God and record His workings through your prayers. Your thirst for Him and growing relationship will only deepen, and at the last, will deliver you and your Kingdom work before the throne of God to receive His praise and great rewards for your labors on earth.

RESOURCES

Barclay, W. (1974). *Education ideals in the ancient world.* Grand Rapids, MI: Baker Book House. (Original work published 1959)

Barclay, W. (2001). *Great themes of the New Testament.* Louisville, KY: Westminster John Knox Press.

Barna, G. (2003, November 17). Research shows that spiritual maturity process should start at a young age. Retrieved March 29, 2009, from http://www.barna.org/barna-update/article/5-barna-update/130-research-shows-that-spiritual-maturity-process-should-start-at-a-young-age

Barna, G. (2006, September 11). Most twentysomethings put Christianity on the shelf following spiritually active teen years. Retrieved from http://www.barna.org/barna-update/article /16-teensnext-gen/147-most-twentysomethings-put-christianity-on-the-shelf-following-spiritually-active-teen-years

Barna, G. (2003). *Transforming children into spiritual champions: Why children should be your church's #1 priority*. Raleigh, NC: Regal House Publishing.

Bavolek, S. J. (Ed.). (2003). *Hardwired to connect: The new scientific case for authoritative community.* Hanover, NH: Dartmouth Medical School Institute for American Values & YMCA of USA.

Beechick, R. (2004). *Heart & mind: What the Bible says about learning.* Fenton, MI: Mott Media, L.L.C.

Bernstein, D. A., Roy, E. J., Srull, T. K., & Wickens, C. D. (1988). *Psychology.* Boston, MA: Houghton-Mifflin.

Berry, C. S. (2009). *Development of a conceptual framework for a biblically derived discipleship model for kingdom education.* Virginia Beach, VA: Regent University.

Bloom, B. S. (1956). *Taxonomy of educational objectives, the classification of educational goals – Handbook I: Cognitive Domain.* New York, NY: McKay.

Brady, M. (2003). *The wisdom of listening.* Boston, MA: Wisdom House.

Brookover, W. B., & Lezotte, L. (1982). *Creating effective schools.* Holmes Beach, FL: Learning Publication.

Catsambis, S. (2007). *Parental involvement in education.* Retrieved February 9, 2009, from Blackwell Reference Online, Blackwell Encyclopedia of Sociology: http://www.blacwellreference.com

Chapman, G. (1997). *The five love languages of children.* Chicago, IL: Northfield.

Chapman, G. (2002). *The love languages of God: How to feel and reflect divine love.* Chicago, IL: Northfield.

Chapman, G. (2005). *The heart of the five love languages.* Chicago, IL: Northfield.

Charney, R., Crawford, L., & Wood, C. (1999). The development of responsibility in early adolescence: Approaches to social and emotional learning in the middle school. In Cohen, J. (Ed.), *Educating minds and hearts: Social emotional learning and the passage into adolescence* (pp. 95-111). New York, NY: Teachers College Press.

Cohen, J. (1999). *Educating minds and hearts: Social emotional learning and the passage into adolescence.* New York, NY: Teachers College Press.

Comer, J.P. (2004). *Leave no child behind.* New Haven, CT: Yale University Press.

Cox, W. F. (2016). *Foundations for a biblically based theory of teaching and learning.* Unpublished manuscript, Regent University, Virginia Beach, VA.

Cox, W. F. (2011). *Kingdom education.* Unpublished work, Regent University, Virginia Beach, VA.

Cox, W. F. (2013). Kingdome education. *Journal of Research on Christian Education, 20*(3), 330-341.

Cox, W. F., Arroyo, A. A., & Bostain, D. (1999). Development of a nurturance teaching model. In D. C. Elliot & S. D. Haltrop (Eds), *Nurturing and reflective teachers* (pp. 129-140). Claremont, CA: Learning Light Educational Consulting and Publishing.

Cox, W. F., & Hameloth, N. (2003-2009). *Holy nation citizenship curriculum.* Virginia Beach, VA: Regent University.

Cox, W. F., Peck, R. A. (2018). Christian education as discipleship formation. *Christian Education Journal, 15*(2), 243-261

Edelmann, S. (2006). *Development of a conceptual framework for a K-12 Christian school curriculum* (Doctoral dissertation). Regent University, Virginia Beach, VA.

Edmonds, R. (1979). Effective schools for the urban poor. *Educational Leadership, 37,* 15-23.

Eisner, E. (2005). Back to whole. *Educational Leadership, 63*(1), 14-18.

Elliot, D. C. (1999). *Nurturing and reflective teachers: A Christian approach for the 21st century.* Claremont, CA: Learning Light Educational Consulting and Publishing.

Emotions. (2010). Retrieved from http://dictionary.com/reference.com/

Erikson, E. H. (1950). *Childhood and society.* New York, NY: W. W. Norton & Co.

Friesen, J. G., Wilder, E. J., Bierling, A., Koepcke, R., & Poole, M. (2000). *The life model: Living from the heart Jesus gave you.* Van Nuys, CA: Shepherd's House.

Gardner, H. (1999). *Intelligence reframed: Multiple intelligences for the 21st century.* New York, NY: Basic Books.

Goleman, D. (1995). *Emotional intelligence: What it is and why it can matter more than IQ.* New York, NY: Bantam Books.

Goleman, D. (2002). *The new leaders: Transforming the art of leadership into the science of results.* London, Emgland: Little, Brown.

Goleman, D. (2006). The socially intelligent leader. *Educational Leadership, 64*(1), 76-81.

Goleman, D., McKee, A., & Bovatis, R. F. (2002). *Primal leadership: Realizing the power of emotional intelligence.* Boston, MA: Harvard Business School Press.

Grimmett, P. & Mackinnon, A. (1992). Craft knowledge and the education of teachers. In G. Grant (Ed.), *Review of research in education,* (Vol. 18, pp. 385-456). Washington, DC: American Educational Research Association.

Hameloth, N. (2007). *Evaluation of holy nation citizenship curriculum.* Unpublished work, Regent University, Virginia Beach, VA.

Hameloth, N. (2011). *Development of a relationship-focused supplement to accompany the holy nation citizenship curriculum for training teachers.* (Doctoral dissertation). Regent University, Virginia Beach, VA.

Harris, A., Day, C., Hadfield, M., Hopkins, D., Hargreave, A., & Chapman, C. (2003). *Effective leadership for school improvement.* New York, NY: RoutledgeFalmer.

Harris, D. N., & Rutledge, S. A. (2007). Models and predictors of teacher effectiveness: A review of the literature with lessons from (and for) other occupations. Retrieved from http://www.teacherqualityresearch.org/models.pdf

Hayford, J. (1995). *The Hayford Bible handbook: The complete companion for Spirit-filled Bible study.* Nashville, TN: Thomas Nelson.

Henry, M. (1706). *Commentary on the whole Bible, volume I (Genesis to Deuteronomy).* Christian Classics Ethereal Library. Retrieved from www.ccel.org/ccel/henry/mhc1.html

Hillsdale College. (n.d.). Philosophy. Retrieved from https://medium.-com/@hillsdale/philosophy-and-the-university.

Kinsey, G. (2006). Understanding the dynamics of No Child Left Behind: Teacher efficacy and support for beginning teachers. *Educational Leadership and Administration, 18,* 147-162.

Kose, B. W. (2007). Principal leadership for social justice: Uncovering the content of teacher professional development. *Journal of School Leadership, 17,* 276-312.

Marlow, D. R. (1977). *Textbook of pediatric nursing* (5th ed.). Philadelphia, PA: W. B. Saunders.

Mazian. (2019). The effect of music on plant growth. Retrieved from https://dengarden.com /gardening/the-effect-of-music-on-plant-growth

Murphy, J., & Hallinger, P. (1985). Effective high schools—What are the common characteristics? *NASSP Bulletin, 69*(477), 18-22.

Nehemiah Institute. (2010). *Links of interest.* Retrieved from http://www.nehemiahinstitute.com /links.php

Ornish, D. (1998). *Love & survival: The scientific basis for the healing power of intimacy.* New York, NY: HarperCollins.

Ornish, D. (2005, October 3). Love is real medicine: Loneliness fosters cardiovascular disease. Fortunately, there's an antidote. *Newsweek, 146*(14), 56.

Palmer, P. (1997). *The heart of a teacher: Identity and integrity in teaching.* Retrieved from http://www.newhorizons.org

Regis University. (2006). Objectives. Retrieved from https://cpslearning.regis.edu/ed_lesson_plan /objectives.html.

Rose, J. B. (1992). *A guide to American Christian education for the home and school* (Bicentennial ed.). San Francisco, CA: Foundation for American Christian Education.

Schutte, P. (2004). *Greek vs Hebrew educational methodology.* Retrieved from http://www.homeschoolbuilding.org/

Scott, D. G. (2000). *The fantasy of organic evlution* (Tract). 1-7.

Seymour, J. L., & Miller, D. E. (1990). *Theological approaches to Christian education.* Nashville, TN: Abingdon Press.

Slater, R. J. (1965/1999). *Teaching and learning America's Christian history: The Principle Approach.* San Francisco, CA: Foundation for American Christian Education.

Strong, J. (1890). *Strong's concordance with Hebrew and Greek lexicon.* Retrieved from http://www.eliyah.com/lexicon.html

Stronge, J. (2002). *Qualities of effective teachers.* Alexandria, VA: Association for Supervision and Curriculum Design.

Stronge, J., Tucker, P., & Hindman, J. L. (2003). *Handbook for qualities of effective teachers.* Alexandria, VA: Association for Supervision and Curriculum Design.

Teddlie, C., & Reynolds, D. (2000). *The international handbook of school effectiveness research.* London: Falmer.

Tirozzi, G.N. (2002). *Reflections on school leadership: A collection of writings and speeches.* Reston, VA: National Association of Secondary School Principals.

Van Brummelen, H. (2002). *Steppingstones to curriculum: A Biblical path.* Colorado Springs, CO: Purposeful Design Pulications.

Van Brummelen, H. (2005). Teachers as servant leaders. *Christian School Education, 8*(3), 20-22.

Webster, N. (1828). *Noah Webster's 1828 dictionary of the American language.* Retrieved from http://www.cbtministries.org/resources/webster1828.htm

Wilson, M. R. (2003). *Our father Abraham.* Dayton, OH: Center for Judaicc-Christian Studies. (Original work published 1989)

Youmans, E. L. (2004). *The Noah plan self-directed study in the Principle Approach.* Chesapeake, VA: Foundation for American Christian Education.

Youmans, E. L. (2001-2016). *Christian view of children.* Retrieved from Chrysalis International: http://www.chrysalisinternational.org/

Yount, W. R. (1999). *Called to teach: An introduction to the ministry of teaching.* Nashville, TN: Broadman & Holman.

ABOUT THE AUTHOR

Dr. Nancy Hameloth resides in Connecticut near her two grown children and three grandchildren. She is an adjunct professor at Regent University in Virginia Beach, VA and Three Rivers Community College in Norwich, CT. She is the founder of B.E.S.T.: Biblical Education Support Training. She has been a Christian school teacher for more than thirty years and has training in the Abeka, Accelerated Christian Education, and Principle Approach curriculum. She also works at Calvary Chapel in Uncasville, CT as the Director of the Connection Ministry. She earned her Bachelor of Arts degree from Central Bible College, her Masters from Pensacola Christian College and Regent University, and her Doctorate from Regent University.

NEXT STEPS

If you have enjoyed this book and would like to continue to train in Kingdom education, here are a few things you can do:

1. Visit our website at: BiblicalEducationSupportTraining.com.

2. Take the course that goes along with this book.

3. Sign up for personal coaching.

Made in the USA
Middletown, DE
30 September 2019